Finance Fairy in High Heels

Wealth Building for Women

by

Scarlett Brooks

Table of Contents

Introduction:
Embracing Your Financial Journey

Welcome to the gateway of financial empowerment, a world where balance sheets and bank statements become as familiar as your favorite coffee order. Imagine a world where discussions around dividends and debt reduction are as comfortable and empowering as conversations about career advancement and personal growth. That world can be yours, and it begins with embracing your financial journey.

Your path to financial wisdom isn't just about crunching numbers; it's a deeply personal voyage that intertwines with every part of your life. This journey, my fellow travelers, will challenge you, reward you, and above all, it's a journey that you won't have to embark upon alone.

Perhaps you're starting fresh in your financial quest, feeling a mix of excitement and apprehension with a dash of bewilderment for good measure. Or maybe you're already on your way, seeking to refine your strategies and reach for new heights. Wherever you stand today, you stand at the threshold of possibility.

Handling finances isn't just a matter of making ends meet. It's about crafting the lifestyle you desire, securing your future, and building a legacy that resonates with your personal values. It's about taking control, making informed decisions, and steering your life towards the destinations you choose.

But let's be real, the world of finance hasn't always been the most inviting place for women. There's a wealth of jargon, an abundance of opinions, and sometimes, a discernible chill when you step into what has historically been a male-dominated field. Here's the good news: the tides are changing, and they're changing because of women like you who are ready to step up and claim their financial power.

This book isn't a simple how-to manual; it's a celebration of your capabilities and a toolkit for your financial success. Whether you're a young professional just starting to navigate the complexities of compensation packages, an entrepreneur trying to fund your dream, or you're approaching retirement and wondering how to ensure a comfortable future – you're in the right place.

Financial fluency is a form of self-care; it's as essential as nurturing your health or cultivating your relationships. When you understand and manage your finances, you give yourself peace of mind, the freedom of choice, and the power to support and protect those you love.

A strong financial foundation enables you to weather storms with grace. It gives you the freedom to say 'no' when you need to and allows you to say 'yes' when opportunities for joy and growth come knocking. It's about being able to make life choices without being overly stressed about the financial impact.

As we venture through these pages together, we'll explore the landscapes of saving with finesse, investing with confidence, and making smart money moves that resonate with your unique life story. And let's not forget the fierce and fabulous side of finances—yes, you can enjoy that designer splurge and still be financially savvy.

Throughout this journey, we'll tackle topics like the psychology of spending and the finesse of negotiating a raise. We'll demystify the stock market and navigate the intricacies of insurance. We'll even delve into the worlds of cryptocurrency, international investing, and the power of philanthropy.

But this book is more than just about personal gain. It's a testament to what we can achieve as individuals and as a collective force. It's about advocating for financial equality, standing as stewards of generational wisdom, and embracing financial technology that keeps us connected and informed.

Imagine a movement where we lift each other up, where your financial freedom becomes a beacon that lights the way for others. This is our call to come together, not just as individual women striving for personal wealth, but as a powerful community igniting change and pioneering progress for all.

So here's to you—the bold, the brilliant, the beautiful. Here's to transforming your relationship with money. Here's to owning your financial narrative and crafting a life that delights and fulfills you.

We're embarking on this journey together; a celebration of wisdom, a commitment to growth, and a toast to the financial future you're about to design. Let's embrace our financial journey with the passion and the resilience it deserves. Your monetary wisdom, like your potential, is limitless. Welcome, to your financial renaissance.

Chapter 1:
Feminine Finance - Understanding Your Money Mindset

Ladies, let's dive into the heart of our financial essence and unravel the tapestry of our money mindsets. Embarking on a journey of economic empowerment starts with a candid look in the mirror, recognizing that our spending habits, savings skills, and investment choices are deeply tinted by who we are and what we believe about money. It's like having a personalized financial fingerprint. This chapter isn't just about numbers and budgets; it's about understanding the 'why' behind your money moves. It's about exploring those silent whispers in your subconscious that influence every dime you earn, save, and spend. To change your financial destiny, it's crucial to dig into your past, present, and future relationship with money. With wisdom, patience, and a sprinkle of tenacity, you'll learn to rewrite your financial story, one empowering chapter at a time.

The Psychology of Spending Let's talk about the psychology of spending, because if we're honest, how we use our money often says a whole lot about who we are. It's like wearing your heart on your sleeve, or in our case, perhaps your wallet. Ever wonder why that gorgeous pair of shoes called out to you, even when you knew your budget was tight? Or why that unplanned splurge at your favorite boutique felt so exhilarating at the moment, yet filled you with regret only hours later?

That's because spending is not just a physical act; it's an emotional one, intertwined with our sense of self, our dreams, and our deepest fears. It's less about the items we're buying and more about the feelings we're chasing. This is critical to recognize, especially as we learn to navigate our financial paths with grace and wisdom.

Your spending habits, believe it or not, start forming early. As a child, you may have watched important figures in your life handle money. Whether they were frugal or free-spirited spenders, their behaviors have likely left an imprint on you. It's not just nurture, though; nature also plays a role. We all have different personality traits that influence how we view and spend money. Some may find comfort in saving, while others experience joy in spending. Understanding these impulses can be the first step to mastering them.

Consider for a moment the power of advertising. The colors, the music, the very words used—they aren't just thrown together; they're carefully crafted to evoke emotion, to create a need where there wasn't one. Why? Because marketers know that emotion drives spending. When something resonates with our aspirations or soothes our insecurities, our grip on rational thought can slip, and we find ourselves reaching for that credit card.

But here's a secret: when you understand these emotions, you can start to control them. That doesn't mean stifling your desires—it means recognizing them for what they are. It means pausing before a purchase and asking, "Is this something that truly aligns with who I am and what I want for my future?" You see, smart spending isn't about restriction; it's about making sure that every dollar you part with brings you closer to your real goals—not just the fleeting satisfaction of an impulse buy.

Speaking of impulse buys, have you noticed how often they happen when we're feeling a certain way? Maybe we're elated and think we deserve a treat, or we're down and looking for a pick-me-up.

Our emotional states are like undercurrents, pulling our spending habits this way and that. It's essential to catch ourselves in those states and develop coping mechanisms that don't involve spending. This might be as simple as a breathing exercise, a walk, or a chat with a friend.

Now, let's address retail therapy. It's real, and for many, it's a coping mechanism for stress, sadness, or even boredom. But is a temporary high worth long-term financial strain? It's time to be as nurturing to our bank accounts as we try to be to our psyches during those tough days. Let's find healthier, more sustainable sources of comfort.

Technology, oh, technology—how you've changed the game! With one-click buying, digital wallets, and never-ending online sales, the barriers between us and spending have all but disappeared. Plus, in a world where social media often sets unrealistic standards of living, the struggle to keep up can lead to serious financial strain. But when armed with awareness and strategies to combat these pressures, you can rewrite the rulebook on your terms.

There's also something to be said about the joy of anticipation. Studies have shown that waiting for something can increase our enjoyment of it. So why rob ourselves of that joy by giving in to instant gratification? Delaying a purchase can not only give us time to assess its true value but can also enhance our enjoyment when we finally do make the decision to spend.

Another layer to the psychology of spending is the concept of value. Not just the price tag on an item, but the personal value we assign to our purchases. We all perceive value differently—a twenty-dollar shirt might mean quality to one person and extravagance to another. By being mindful of what we truly value, we become intentional with our spending, and every purchase becomes a reflection of what matters most to us.

So, how do we work with our psychology to cultivate healthier spending habits? It starts with setting clear financial goals, which we'll be exploring more deeply in upcoming chapters. Goals give spending a purpose and a direction, rather than letting it run wild and aimless. They set the stage for strategic choices that align with our larger life vision.

And let's not forget peer pressure. It doesn't only affect teenagers—it's alive and thriving among adults, too. Whether it's dinners out, vacations, or material possessions, the desire to fit in can take a toll on our wallets. Standing in our financial truth requires courage, but it also builds resilience and authenticity. By defining our ideas of success and luxury, we can stand confidently in our financial decisions without being swayed by the crowd.

In the end, each of us has the power to rewrite our financial stories. By understanding the psychological forces behind our spending, we can begin to build a relationship with money that's empowering, enriching, and deliberate. So, as we dive deeper into the tools and strategies that'll help us thrive financially, let's keep in mind that it's not just about discipline. It's about crafting a thoughtful, passionate approach to money—one that honors who we are and all that we aspire to be.

Building a Healthy Financial Self-Image is as essential as establishing a savings account or planning for retirement. Your mindset plays a pivotal role in how you perceive and handle your finances. It sets the foundation for your financial decisions and ultimately your financial well-being. Let's dive deep into how you can nurture a positive financial self-image that empowers you to take control of your money narrative.

First things first - your self-worth is not measured by your net worth. Understanding this distinction is key to building a healthy financial self-image. Yes, money is important, it helps you live the life you want, but it's not the core of who you are. What you own or earn doesn't define your value as a person or your capabilities. Begin by acknowledging your intrinsic worth and remind yourself that financial success is a journey you're committed to, not a destination.

Let's shift our focus to positive self-talk. The discussion around money can often feel laden with guilt or shame, especially if we're just getting to grips with financial basics or if we've stumbled in the past. Positive affirmations can help rewire these thought patterns. Practice saying things like, "I am capable of making smart financial choices," or, "I am learning and growing with my finances every day." These small yet potent statements help build a framework for a self-assured approach to money management.

It's also important to celebrate all wins, no matter how small. Paid off a credit card? Give yourself a high-five. Saved up for that special purchase without going into debt? You're awesome! Recognizing these milestones is essential for developing a sense of financial competence and accomplishment. Tracking progress is not just about figures on a balance sheet - it's about honoring the hard work that got you there.

Now, let's talk about the power of visualization. Have you ever imagined what financial independence looks and feels like to you? Is it the freedom to travel, the ability to support loved ones, or perhaps the security of a fully-funded retirement account? Whatever it is, picturing your financial goals can serve as a powerful motivator and reaffirm that you're on the right path. Visualization reinforces your financial goals and embeds them into your subconscious, working as a map towards your intended destination.

Understanding that knowledge is power plays a critical role in shaping a sound financial self-image. The world of finance can seem overwhelming, but it's essential to be a lifelong learner. Take courses, read books, listen to podcasts - absorb information that will enhance your financial literacy. Each new piece of knowledge is a tool that sharpens your ability to make informed decisions, thereby improving your financial confidence.

It's also crucial to surround yourself with a supportive community. Discussions about money shouldn't be taboo, and finding like-minded individuals who are transparent about their financial journeys can be incredibly uplifting. There's immense value in learning from others' experiences. A community can offer encouragement, share resources, and provide a network for accountability as you work towards enhancing your financial narrative.

An unwavering part of building a healthy financial self-image is setting boundaries. This may mean learning to say no to certain expenses to prioritize your financial goals or establishing limits on how much you lend to others. Remember, safeguarding your financial health is not selfish - it's smart and necessary for long-term stability.

Dealing with setbacks with grace is equally important. The road to financial empowerment is rarely without bumps. Whether it's an unexpected expense or a market downturn, view these challenges as learning opportunities rather than disasters. By taking setbacks in stride and maintaining a solution-focused attitude, you're building resilience and a realistic yet optimistic financial self-image.

Don't underestimate the value of a robust financial plan. This plan is akin to a personal roadmap; it tells you where you are and guides you to where you want to go. A clear, actionable plan helps you visualize your financial goals, outlines the steps to get there, and serves as a constant reminder that you are working towards something meaningful. Plus, it's a tangible reflection of your financial acumen and commitment.

Fostering gratitude is another gem in nurturing a healthy financial self-image. Being grateful for what you currently have sets a tone of contentment and abundance. It lets you focus on wealth rather than lack, providing an affirmative backdrop for financial decisions and attracting more positivity into your life.

Reflection is a powerful tool. Take time to reflect on your financial journey - the decisions you've made, the habits you've formed, and the knowledge you've gained. Reflecting helps you recognize patterns, celebrate growth, and course-correct where necessary. Think of it as a financial self-checkup that ensures you're aligned with your values and goals.

Part of building a sound financial self-image also involves controlling the narrative. You might come across naysayers or traditional beliefs that challenge your financial autonomy. Stand firm in your convictions and craft a money story that resonates with you, not one dictated by societal pressures or outdated norms. Yours is a narrative of empowerment, intelligence, and resolve.

Maintaining transparency with yourself about money matters is essential. Often, we might try to avoid looking at our finances out of fear or uncertainty. However, being honest about your financial situation is the first step to improvement. Embrace your current financial state with openness, and use it as your baseline for growth.

Lastly, celebrate yourself as a whole. Remember, you're not just a saver, spender, or earner; you're a multifaceted being with diverse talents and dreams. Embracing all aspects of yourself, including your financial facet, contributes to comprehensive self-esteem and reinforces a strong, well-rounded self-image.

In conclusion, crafting a healthy financial self-image is a mix of mindset, education, resilience, and self-respect. It's about setting and celebrating milestones, embracing the learning curve, and standing tall in your financial story. Nurture it like an investment that pays dividends in confidence, clarity, and independence. It's time to weave financial empowerment into the fabric of your identity and let your financial self-image shine with the strength and grace you possess.

Chapter 2:
The Power of the Purse - Setting Financial Goals

Having dusted off your money mindset in Chapter 1, it's time to dive into the heart of financial empowerment: setting your financial goals. Let's face it, goals are the fuel propelling you towards that luscious life of financial freedom. They're not just daydreams; they're your future reality with a deadline. Think about what you truly want—a vacation, a home, a cushy retirement—and let's map out how to grab it. Consider this chapter your financial fairy godmother, transforming vague wishes into actionable, concrete financial targets. We're not just talking about any old goals; we're crafting a high-end, designer portfolio of dreams with practical, achievable steps forward. Imagine seamlessly weaving short-term triumphs with a long-term vision that spells out 'success' on your terms. No cookie-cutter advice here, just a savvy blueprint tailored to your life's desires, plotted with precision and ready to burst into glorious fruition. Embrace your ambitions and let's cultivate that power of the purse, making every dollar count and every dream a plan in the making.

Short-Term Wins and Long-Term Vision Transitioning into the groove of managing finances, let's illuminate the pathway to both immediate gratification and a prosperous future. Imagine the feeling when you check off a goal on your list. That's the euphoria of a short-term win! They can be as simple as cutting back on daily coffee runs or learning to negotiate bills, but the impact is tangible. These quick victories are essential—they fuel our dedication and propel us towards the more grandiose ambitions that we all harbor. Yes, that long-term vision you hold dear, whether it's owning a serene beachside bungalow or commanding a boardroom, is utterly attainable. Let's dive into how these wins will guide you there.

So, what makes these short-term wins so vital to our journey? For one, they're motivators. By celebrating small successes, we validate our strategy and build the confidence to tackle larger objectives. Think of them as the sparkles that keep your financial journey dazzling. Seen a reduction in your credit card debt? Applaud yourself! Every penny you save today is a step toward that ultimate vision you desire.

However, without marrying these quick wins to a long-term vision, they can evoke fleeting joy. It's like wearing the latest trend—it's awesome now, but without a timeless piece in your wardrobe, you're left unprepared for the future. A clear long-term vision creates a roadmap, directing your decisions and giving context to your short-term goals.

Let's dissect this vision concept. At its core, it's the blueprint of your heart's aspirations when it comes to wealth. Envision where you want to be financially in 10, 20, or 30 years. Although it can seem like a marathon, this vision isn't static; it should evolve as you grow, empowering you to adapt yet stay focused on the bigger picture. Crafting this vision requires introspection—understand what truly matters to you and let that shape your financial future.

Crafting a long-term vision might start broad, like saying you want to 'travel the world' or 'be debt-free'. Yet these are the seeds from which you can cultivate a detailed plan. Break down that globe-trotting dream into steps. Perhaps next year's goal is visiting the vineyards of Tuscany, and five years later, it's a safari in Africa. Money is the vessel that will carry you to these experiences. By linking each short-term win to these milestones, the journey becomes part of the thrill.

Implementing short-term financial wins is no less than a savvy shopping spree—you're investing in a bargain that's bound to appreciate over time. Maybe it's starting a side hustle, learning to invest, or setting aside a small amount monthly into a high-yield savings account. The key is to create a routine that generates these wins regularly, turning them into the stepping stones towards your financial sovereignty.

Acknowledging our wins can sometimes feel indulgent, but it's far from it. Celebrate every achievement, each positive shift in behavior or strategy adjustment. Did you mitigate an impulsive purchase? Go you! Celebrating progress instills a positive financial culture within yourself, making it more likely for you to commit to your vision in the long run.

Nevertheless, while short-term wins offer a buzz, let's not forget that long-term vision demands consistency. Like cultivating a rare orchid, patience is crucial. The realignment of your plans could be necessary as circumstances change, but keeping your eyes on that prize will ensure continuous progress. It's about striking that balance—relishing in your immediate triumphs while steadfastly advancing toward your future affluence.

But how do we practically intertwine these short-term wins with our overarching vision? By setting milestones along the way—like mini celebrations. These are the landmarks that will remind you of the journey's joy. Setting and achieving concrete benchmarks keeps the 'financial flame' alive, making each step forward a testimony to your evolving acumen.

And while we're headed towards our goals, let's talk budgeting. It may sound plain, but think of it as designing a couture dress; it's tailored to your financial body. Budgeting is the art of knowing your limits while still enjoying life's pleasures. Allocating funds specifically for quick wins alongside long-term goals is essential, making sure they coexist harmoniously rather than compete.

Reflect on making wise investments as part of your long-term vision. It could be investing in education to boost your earning potential or buying stocks in a start-up. The right choices can transform your financial canvas from blank to colorful, each stroke representing a wise move you've made on the immediacy of today and the posterity of tomorrow.

As a financially astute woman, the magnitude of negotiating should never be underestimated. Be it haggling down a cable bill or negotiating your salary, these feats serve dual purposes. Not only do they result in short-term advantages, but they also set a precedent for future financial interactions. It's about gaining value now, which compounds over time.

Remember, the long-term vision is more than a dream—it's a commitment to yourself. It should inspire you, push you through tough days, and remind you why every financial decision matters. What's more, this vision isn't for anyone else—it's wholly, authentically, unapologetically yours. Own it, shape it, and you will be amazed at where you can go.

Let's not forget, the support of a community, perhaps a network of like-minded women, bolsters both short-term and long-term progress. Share your victories, seek advice, and harness the collective wisdom that only a community can provide. The insights you'll gain are invaluable in refining your vision and strategies.

So, as we look ahead, remember that the coalescence of short-term wins and a steadfast long-term vision is the essence of a financially empowered woman. Each win, no matter how small, is a piece of the puzzle that shapes your future. And your vision, that glamorous, bold, and unyielding dream, is worth every effort. Keep your eyes poised on the horizon and your ledger grounded in the present, and watch as your financial tapestry becomes a masterpiece of personal achievement and autonomy.

SMART Goals for Financial Success As we've laid the groundwork for financial empowerment, let's pivot to one of the most potent instruments you'll employ: SMART goals. These precise, measurable, achievable, relevant, and time-bound goals are your roadmap to financial success. Crafting SMART goals isn't just about jotting down dreams—it's about creating a plan that will take you from where you are now to where you want to be.

Imagine standing at the base of a mountain, eager to reach its peak. Without a path marked out, the trek could be overwhelming, if not impossible. That's akin to striving for financial success without SMART goals—they are your trail markers, your checkpoints, your guide to the summit of your financial Everest. Whether it's saving for a down payment on a house, setting aside funds for a sabbatical, or building an ample nest egg for retirement, let's delve into how you can intelligently frame your ambitions.

Firstly, make your goals *specific*. A goal stating, "I want to save money" is like setting sail without a compass. Refine it. How much do you want to save? Why? Rather than a vague intention, a specific goal would be, "I want to save $10,000 for a down payment on a condo." Suddenly, you've got a target.

Next, ensure your goals are *measurable*. Track your progress by standardizing your ambitions. If your aim is to save $10,000 in two years, break it down. That means you need to save about $417 every month. Now, you have a way to measure and mold your habits month by month.

Aiming high is fantastic, but your goals also need to be *achievable*. Setting the bar sky-high—such as having a goal to save a million dollars in two years with a moderate income—might leave you dispirited. Conversely, a goal should stretch you slightly so you feel challenged. "I will contribute 15% of my monthly earnings to my retirement

16

account" might be a sturdy goal that stretches your financial discipline muscles without causing strain.

Relevance is where the heart comes in. Your goals should align with your values and your long-term vision. A goal that's important to you will fuel your motivation. Maybe you're passionate about travel, so saving for a round-the-world trip could resonate more than saving for the latest car model.

Finally, each goal should be *time-bound*. A deadline acts as a motivator; it's the difference between setting out for an afternoon hike and an aimless wander. Plan timeframes for your goals—a timeline brings a sense of urgency and helps prioritize your daily activities in line with your goals.

With your SMART goals sketched out, get into the habit of revisiting them frequently. This could mean weekly check-ins or a monthly financial "date" with yourself to review and adjust as necessary. Life is fluid, circumstances change, and your goals may need to ebb and flow as well.

To power up your goal-setting, visualize your success. Create a vision board or write a detailed narrative of your life with your goals achieved. How will it feel? What will change? Use these images and emotions to keep the fire of ambition burning, even on days when motivation wanes.

Build a support network for your goals. Like-minded friends or a mentor can offer invaluable encouragement and accountability. Sharing your goals with someone else solidifies your commitment and can inspire you to push through challenges.

Up next, deal with potential setbacks proactively. If you face an obstacle, revisit your goals, identify what the roadblock is, and brainstorm solutions. Resilience is a key ingredient in the recipe for financial success.

Don't be shy to celebrate your successes, no matter how small. Achieving a milestone reinforces your behavior and provides positive reinforcement. Did you just reach the halfway point of your savings goal? Indulge in a little celebration—it's a powerful way to honor your progress.

Autonomy is vital. Remember, these are your goals, so they should be chosen and defined by you. They're not your parent's goals, your partner's, nor society's—this is your financial journey. Owning your goals translates to a deeper commitment to fulfilling them.

Resourcefulness also plays a role. There may be financial concepts or tools that can fast-track your path to your goals. Don't hesitate to seek out knowledge and resources. Books, online courses, financial planning apps or even professional financial advice could open up new avenues for success.

In the spirit of being SMART, stay flexible. Goals can change, and that's okay. The important thing is that you adjust them in a way that continues to align with your overarching vision. Financial success isn't a static end goal; it's a dynamic, ongoing process.

By incorporating the SMART framework into your financial planning, you'll be poised to progress with confidence. Each successful goal brings you one step closer to the financial independence and mastery you're striving for. It's not just about having a full bank account; it's about the freedom, choice, and peace of mind that come with it.

Ladies, as we traverse the terrain of our financial landscapes, let's do so methodically and SMARTly. Here's to setting goals as brilliant and bold as you are—and achieving each one with grace, grit, and unwavering determination.

Chapter 3:
Budgets and Louboutins - Crafting Your Spending Plan

So, you've acknowledged the power wallet wields and set some killer goals—it's time to sculpt a spending plan as sassy and smart as you are. Picture your budget as the map to your financial independence, every line guiding your cash flow with intention and purpose, without skimping on the glam. Think of it this way: every dollar has its destiny, whether that's towards savings, investment, or yes, those fabulous red-soled Louboutins that make your heart sing. This chapter is about embracing the elegance of practicality; it's not just about crunching numbers but about crafting a personal spending philosophy that honors both your day-to-day needs and your plush, plush dreams. It's about finding freedom within a framework—being as conscious about paying the electricity bill as you are about investing in those statement pieces that define your style. By the end of this section, you'll not only revel in the relief that comes with a well-tailored budget but also stride with the confidence of a woman who knows her financial footing—in high heels, no less.

The Basics of Budgeting As we step into the realm of shaping our financial futures, it's time we talk about one of the most foundational elements: budgeting. A budget isn't just a way to track your expenses; it's the financial reflection of your priorities, dreams, and hard work. Let's begin the transformative journey towards financial independence with the simple act of understanding what comes in, what goes out, and most importantly, why.

Picture your finances as a garden. To flourish, it needs regular care and the right balance of nutrients and water. Think of budgeting as the gardening plan you craft, outlining where to plant, how much to water, and what areas need the most attention. To start, dig into your income - the sunlight that powers your financial garden. Know your net income, the actual amount that lands in your bank account after taxes and deductions. This figure is the starting point of any budget.

Next, let's talk about expenses. Fixed expenses, like rent or a mortgage, are the perennial plants of our garden. Predictable, steady, and necessary. Variable expenses, on the other hand, are akin to the annuals - food, entertainment, and shopping - adding variety but requiring more flexible care. Tracking these for a couple of months will bring clarity to your financial landscape and reveal the true nature of your spending habits.

With the basics laid out, begin drafting your budget. You can't miss the 50/30/20 rule as a guiding principle, allocating 50% of your income to needs, 30% to wants, and 20% to savings and debt repayment. Yet, remember, this is simply a template. Tailor it to the lifestyle you envision for yourself. Maybe your goals demand a 40/20/40 structure - and that's absolutely fine. Your budget must fit you like a perfectly tailored dress - unique and flattering to your financial shape.

Be hands-on and detailed with your budget. Allocate every dollar a job, ensuring that your spending aligns with your values and goals. It's like deciding which events to grace with your presence - some are must-attends, while others may not make the cut. And when life throws a gala or two your way, be prepared with a "miscellaneous" category, so these surprises don't ruffle your feathers.

Remember, a budget is not set in stone. It's an adjustable map that helps you navigate your financial journey. As life evolves, so should your budget. Just like fashion trends, you keep what works and revamp what doesn't. Regularly review and recalibrate your spending plan to ensure it continues to serve your changing life.

Automation can be a powerful ally in your budgeting strategy. Setting up automatic transfers to savings accounts or bill payments ensures that your financial commitments are met without you lifting a finger. Think of it like a subscription service to your future self - it takes care of the essentials, so you're free to bask in the present.

But what happens when the budget shows you're living beyond your means? Then, it's time to take a hard look at your expenses and pinpoint areas for trimming. Dining out, subscription services, or the occasional indulgence in retail therapy - these are often the first spots where you can regain control. It's about making intentional choices, not cutting out joy from your life.

And don't underestimate the power of negotiation. Many fixed expenses, such as phone bills or insurance premiums, can often be lowered with a simple call. Arm yourself with research and the confidence that asking for better rates is not only smart but an act of self-respect for your financial well-being.

Savings should have a VIP spot in your budget. Even if it starts small, prioritize contributing to your emergency fund and retirement savings. These are your financial safety net and golden ticket to future freedom. Treat them like the exclusive spa retreats for your money – places where it can relax and grow undisturbed.

And as you embrace budgeting, let it be known that setbacks are a part of the process. Perhaps a sudden expense throws your budget off track, but don't let that spell defeat. Adjust, learn, and move forward.

It's the resilience in refining your budget that'll sharpen your financial acumen.

Enlist the aid of technology to streamline your budgeting. Plenty of apps and tools offer user-friendly interfaces and valuable insights into your personal finances. These digital assistants can take the tedium out of tracking expenses, making it easier for you to stick to your budget and spot trends over time.

Surround yourself with inspiration. Seek out stories of other women who've successfully managed their finances. Learn from their experiences and let their victories fuel your determination. Remember, you're not alone on this journey, and there's a wealth of collective wisdom to tap into.

Lastly, don't forget to budget for fun. Money is a tool, and while it's crucial to plan for the future, it's equally important to enjoy the fruits of your labor now. Allocate funds for those experiences that sprinkle joy into your life – because, in the end, a budget should enable, not restrict, the richness of your life's tapestry.

As we wrap up the basics of budgeting, remember that this is your starting line, not the finish. It's the blueprint for building a stable, prosperous, and joyful financial future. As you turn your attention to each dollar and decision, do so with the understanding that you're crafting not just a budget, but a complete financial story that mirrors your ambition, compassion, and sophistication. Onward, to a pathway where your every financial step is walked with intention, elegance, and confidence.

Stretching Your Dollar with Style Who says that being fiscally responsible means sacrificing your love for the finer things in life? Not here, not us. We're going to dive into ways to make your money go further while still indulging in the elegance and style that make life a little sweeter. It's about smart spending, not no spending, and aligning your financial practices with your personal flair.

Think about quality over quantity. It's tempting to fill your closet or home with items that are trendy or on sale, but these can often lead to more clutter and less satisfaction in the long run. A focus on purchasing fewer, higher quality items not only can give you a sense of luxury but also tends to be a wiser investment. More durable, classic pieces that last for years can actually save you money and hassle over time.

Another savvy move is rethinking where you shop. Consider exploring consignment stores, thrift shops, and online marketplaces for pre-loved luxury items. These treasures can often be found at a fraction of their original price, allowing you to adorn yourself and your home with high-end goods while staying within your budget.

The art of negotiation isn't just for the boardroom; it extends to your everyday purchases as well. Whether you're subscribing to a service or buying a piece of furniture, don't shy away from asking for a better deal. Retailers often have unadvertised discounts or can be flexible on price to make a sale. Remember, the worst they can say is no, and then you're no worse off than before.

When it comes to life's luxuries, timing can be everything. A stunning piece of jewelry or those fabulous designer shoes you've been eyeing will likely go on sale at some point. Patience pays off in these scenarios. Sign up for alerts from your favorite retailers, or use price-tracking tools online to notify you when the cost drops.

It's easy to overlook the power of DIY, but creating your own beauty products, home decor, or even gifts can inject your personal style into every facet of life while keeping your wallet happy. With countless tutorials available online, pursuing DIY projects can be a fulfilling and economically sound hobby.

Reward programs and cash-back offers can give you a bit of luxury for less. It's like getting paid to pamper yourself. So, make sure you're signed up for loyalty programs at places where you regularly shop or services you use often. Always check for cash-back offers when online shopping through browser extensions or cash-back websites. These small amounts can add up to significant savings or even free items.

Dining out and socializing are important for our well-being, but they can add up quickly. An alternative is to host intimate gatherings at home. With some creativity in the kitchen and a knack for ambiance, you can create memorable experiences that rival those pricey nights out. Plus, potluck dinners with friends bring variety to the table and share the cost.

Technology also has a stylish role in thriftiness. Use apps and tools to track price drops, find coupons, compare prices, and even manage your budget. With the right app, you feel like you have a savvy shopping assistant in your pocket, guiding you towards the best deals so you can maintain your fabulous lifestyle without overspending.

Personal style isn't just about what you buy; it's also about how you use what you have. Mix and match your clothing or home decor to keep things fresh. Learning a few basic sewing techniques to tailor your clothes can make an off-the-rack piece look custom-made for you. Redecorate by rearranging furniture or swapping out accent pieces seasonally to rejuvenate your space.

Wellness doesn't need a high price tag. Yoga, meditation, and fitness routines are available for free online. Investing in your health by utilizing these resources, perhaps complemented by a few quality pieces of equipment or stylish workout gear purchased wisely, can reinforce your commitment to both physical and fiscal fitness.

When looking to travel in style, flexibility is key. Being open to off-season getaways, staying in boutique hotels instead of chains, or even opting for daytime flights can make for unforgettable experiences that are gentle on the purse. Travel points and miles accrued through credit cards or loyalty programs can also grant you that luxury vacation you've been dreaming of.

Education is another area where you can economize without compromising on quality. Audiobooks, ebooks, and online courses are often available at a fraction of the cost of traditional media or in-person classes. They also offer the flexibility of learning at your own pace while still gaining valuable knowledge and skills in high style.

Maintaining your financial health is much like maintaining a healthy diet. Indulging every once in a while is absolutely fine – and encouraged! But balance is key. Reward yourself for reaching financial milestones with experiences or items that enhance your style and zest for life without derailing your financial goals.

Lastly, never underestimate the power of saving. 'Save first and spend what's left' isn't just advice; it's a lifestyle worth embracing. Design a luxurious-looking savings jar or a high-style spreadsheet to track your progress. This visual representation can serve as a chic reminder of your journey toward both financial security and a life rich with style.

In the grand canvas of your financially savvy life, there's ample room for creative strokes that add vibrancy without causing overspend. With these tips, you can cultivate a life that's rich in taste and sound in money matters. So here's to making every dollar work as hard as you do, but in the most stylish way possible.

Chapter 4:
Saving with Sophistication -
Mastering the Art of Saving

Stashing away your hard-earned cash isn't just about putting pennies in a piggy bank; it's an exquisite art form that, when mastered, can transform your financial canvas. Imagine crafting a safety net so robust, life's curveballs can't knock you off your fabulous heels. This chapter is about turning the mundane act of saving into a shrewd stratagem where every dollar you tuck away works tirelessly for you. Here, we'll unveil savvy habits to build that emergency fund—because let's be honest, flat tires and leaky roofs have no respect for our schedules. We'll also dive into guilt-free strategies for saving towards those sparkling indulgences that make life extra glossy. It's about creating a balance that allows for both security and splurges, all without breaking a sweat. You'll learn how to make your money multiply in the background, so you can focus on living your most glamorous life upfront. It's time to weave some sophistication into your savings plan and watch your financial confidence skyrocket!

Creating an Emergency Fund Life is full of surprises, and not all of them are pleasant. A sudden job loss, unexpected medical bills, or a major car repair can throw a wrench into the most carefully laid financial plans. That's why having an emergency fund is a non-negotiable foundation of financial health. It's your financial safety net, and building it is one of the smartest moves you can make.

First, let's demystify what an emergency fund actually is—it's a stash of money set aside to cover those unanticipated expenses that life throws your way. This fund keeps you from having to take on debt when you're in a pinch. And here's a powerful truth: being prepared with an emergency fund can provide you with peace of mind that is priceless.

So, how much should you aim to save? While the rule of thumb is to have enough to cover three to six months of living expenses, the exact amount can vary based on your life situation. Are you the sole provider for your household? Do you work in a volatile industry? Adjust your target accordingly. But remember, something is always better than nothing. Even a $500 starter fund can get you out of many a tight spot.

Now, let's talk strategy. Begin by opening a separate savings account for your emergency fund. Why separate? Keeping it distinct from your daily checking account reduces the temptation to dip into it for non-emergencies. You want this fund to be accessible, but not too accessible.

Building up your emergency fund can seem daunting, but it's all about taking it one step at a time. Start with small, manageable goals. Can you set aside $20 each week? How about skipping that extra coffee or lunch out and redirecting that cash to your emergency stash instead? Small amounts can add up big over time.

Automation is your friend here, making saving practically effortless. Many banks offer the option to automatically transfer funds to your savings account on a regular basis. Set up a standing order to sweep money into your emergency fund every payday, and watch your safety net expand without having to think about it.

Raises and bonuses are excellent opportunities to bolster your emergency fund. Resist the urge to spend that unexpected windfall and allocate at least a portion of it to your emergency savings. After all, the best time to save is when you have extra cash flowing in.

What if you're starting from scratch and budgeting is tight? It's time to get creative. Maybe you have skills that could bring in extra income through a side hustle. Every cent you earn on top of your regular income could be channeled into building your emergency fund. Your future self will thank you.

Remember: consistency is key. Even on a tight budget, make saving for your emergency fund a priority. Before long, you'll find that you're building resilience into your financial life. Celebrate each milestone to keep motivated. When you hit $500, do a little dance. Reach $1,000, and give yourself a pat on the back.

Of course, it's one thing to build an emergency fund and another to maintain it. If you need to use it (and that's what it's there for), make sure to replenish it as soon as you're able. It's a cycle — spend on emergencies, rebuild, and repeat as necessary. This ensures you're always prepared for life's unexpected events.

What about those times you're tempted to use your fund for something that's not exactly an emergency? Pause and ask yourself if this expense is truly unexpected and urgent. The fund is there for real emergencies, like a sudden job loss or an immediate home repair, not a spur-of-the-moment vacation or that trendy bag that just went on sale. Discipline is what allows your emergency fund to serve its purpose.

Another thing to consider is where you're keeping this money. Look for a high-yield savings account that offers better interest rates than standard accounts. Your emergency fund should be growing, albeit slowly, even when you're not actively contributing to it.

One of the most empowering things about having an emergency fund is the control it gives you over your own destiny. With this financial buffer, you're not at the mercy of creditors, or forced to borrow from friends or family. It's a symbol of your independence and commitment to taking care of yourself, no matter what happens.

Let's be clear: an emergency fund is not a luxury; it's a necessity. Whether you're a young professional just starting out, an entrepreneur facing the unpredictability of business, or a pre-retiree securing your future, an emergency fund is a foundational piece in the puzzle of your financial independence.

Last but not least, applaud yourself for every step you take toward financial security. Each dollar saved is a brick in the fortress protecting your financial future. Building and maintaining an emergency fund is a testament to your resilience, foresight, and self-respect. Embrace the journey, your safety net is being woven with each wise decision you make.

Saving for Life's Luxuries - stepping into this chapter, let's hone in on a delightful aspect of financial planning: Saving for Life's Luxuries. Envisioning those designer shoes, the sparkle of fine jewelry, or perhaps sipping cocktails on a pristine beach during a dream vacation. Isn't it alluring? Absolutely, but these dreams don't come to fruition by mere wishing; they require a savvy savings strategy.

Now, first off, to save for these coveted items and experiences, you've got to make room in your budget. Yes, the one we've carefully crafted with a place for everything, including occasional splurges. This isn't about overthrowing your current financial plan, but enhancing it with targeted savings for the luxuries that light up your eyes.

Start by defining what a 'luxury' truly is for you. This isn't just about high price tags; it's about significant personal value. Whether it's first-class travel or a state-of-the-art kitchen remodel, pinpoint the extravagances that resonate with your version of a rich, joyful life.

Once you've identified these treasures, set up a dedicated savings account for each. This separation method will keep your luxury funds from getting tangled with other savings goals like emergency funds or retirement. Labeling accounts with their intended purpose can also be incredibly motivating; it's easier to save for a "Paris Getaway" than a nondescript "Savings Account."

Determine the cost of your luxury items or experiences, then break down that lump sum into manageable, monthly savings goals. It might mean sacrificing a few smaller indulgences now, but remember, it's in the service of something bigger and better. You're trading in the instant gratification for a reward that's truly splendid.

One effective technique is to set up automatic transfers to your luxury savings account right after you get paid. It's a form of "paying yourself first" for the delightful extras in life. If the money isn't sitting in your checking account, you're less likely to spend it on other things.

There's something to be said for patience. Delaying your gratification can be tough, especially when you're bombarded with the siren calls of sales and the latest trends. But stay the course. If necessary, unfollow brands and influencers that tempt you to stray from your luxurious goals. Keep your eyes on the prize.

In the meantime, seek out alternative activities that don't cost much but still bring joy. Maybe it's a picnic in the park with friends or an at-home spa day. These can fill the void when you're feeling impatient for your luxury savings to grow.

While you're playing the waiting game, research ways to make your luxury more affordable. Maybe it's timing the purchase to coincide with a sale, buying pre-owned, or using credit card points towards a high-end experience. There's always a smarter way to get what you want for less, without compromising on quality.

If your luxury requires a hefty sum, consider a side hustle to boost your savings rate. Whether that's freelance work, a part-time job, or selling crafts, use your skills and passions to fast-track your way to indulgence.

And yes, there might be setbacks. An unexpected expense could require tapping into your luxury savings. Don't let guilt or frustration derail you. Adjust your timeline, bolster your emergency fund to withstand future surprises, and keep moving forward.

Remember to celebrate milestones along the way to keep your motivation burning. When you're halfway to affording those Italian leather boots or that fine dining experience, treat yourself to a little something to mark the occasion. But keep it sensible; don't undo your hard work!

Sharing your luxury goals with an accountability partner can also help keep you on track. This could be a friend, family member, or even an online community of like-minded individuals. They can offer support, ideas, and perhaps share their own experiences in luxury savings.

When the moment arrives, and you've saved enough to afford your luxury, enjoy it to the fullest. This purchase is more than a mere item or experience; it's a testament to your dedication and financial savvy. Savor the triumph of delayed gratification and remember the journey that led you here.

Last but not least, always consider the impact of your luxury purchases on your overall financial health. Being able to afford life's finer things is not just about the savings in the bank, but also about not compromising your financial future. Ensure that your indulgence aligns with your broader financial goals and doesn't put you at any risk.

By strategically saving for life's luxuries, you're designing a life that's both financially responsible and rich with experiences that truly matter to you. It's about balance, foresight, and a touch of discipline. You've got the financial tools and inner power to bring life's luxuries into your grasp without disrupting your path to financial independence.

Chapter 5:
Debt in Designer Heels -
Managing and Eliminating Debt

Let me tell you, the moment you decide to slip off those debt-ridden designer heels and step into a life of financial freedom is nothing short of empowering. Managing and eliminating debt isn't just about getting back into the black; it's an act that screams independence and control. And it's not about cutting up your cards or living off ramen noodles either. See, we're building a financial runway where you can strut with confidence, understanding that debt can be a savvy leverage tool when used wisely, but a ball and chain when it's not. We'll tackle good debt, bad debt, and the not-so-ugly strategies to pay down what you owe without losing your zest for life. So, let's dive into smart systems to prioritize your debts, negotiate better rates, and create payment plans that don't feel like a straitjacket. It's all about making your money work for you, as you high-step past interest fees and towards a glamorous, debt-free existence.

Understanding Different Types of Debt As we step further into our shared journey of financial fluency, it's time to pull back the curtain on a topic that often causes furrowed brows – debt. Yes, the 'D' word can send shivers down the spine, but it doesn't have to be a nemesis. Knowledge is power, and understanding the various debt types is like arming yourself with a wardrobe that has an outfit for every occasion.

Let's start with the basics: not all debt is created equal. Some can even be downright chic – a strategic accessory to your financial portfolio – while others are the equivalent of wearing socks with sandals: avoidable. The key is discernment, differentiating between what's favorable and what's not.

First, there's good debt. Think of it as your reliable little black dress. It's the kind that, managed well, can help you build wealth or increase your net worth over time. Student loans, for instance, can be considered good debt because they are an investment in your education, which can lead to higher earning potential. Similarly, a mortgage for a home can also be good debt, as it may lead to home equity growth and provide a roof over your head.

However, good debt still requires attention – like making sure your LBD fits impeccably. It's vital to manage these debts prudently, ensuring payments are affordable and interest rates are competitive. Extra points if you can make additional payments to reduce the term and save on interest.

Then we have bad debt. This type can be likened to those flashy, once-worn shoes that now collect dust in the closet. High-interest credit cards and payday loans fit into this category. They often charge exorbitant interest rates and can trap you in a cycle of borrowing more to pay off existing debt, damaging your financial health in the long run.

The best way to handle bad debt? Attack it with the same fervor you'd use to declutter your wardrobe. Make a plan to pay off these debts as quickly as possible. Look for strategies to pay more than the minimum and consider transferring balances to lower interest rate accounts if that option is available to you.

Next on our fashion parade is secured debt. Picture this as the well-tailored coat, providing warmth but requiring a valuable item as collateral. Mortgages and auto loans fall into this category. Because the lender can seize the asset if payments are missed, they often come with lower interest rates than unsecured debts.

On the flip side are unsecured debts - consider these the flashy costume jewelry of finance. These include most credit cards and personal loans without collateral. Although they're easier to obtain, they typically come with higher interest rates, reflecting the higher risk to the lender.

Revolving debt is the versatile wrap dress of your financial closet – flexible and adaptable. Credit cards and lines of credit let you borrow up to a certain limit, pay it off, and borrow again. To keep this flexibility beneficial, it's critical to manage these lines of credit responsibly and avoid the temptation to overextend.

Installment debt is more like the structured winter coat: predictable and steady. It involves borrowing a fixed amount and repaying it in regular installments over a set period. This can include personal loans, auto loans, and mortgages. Stick to the schedule, and you'll stay snugly on track.

Now, let's not forget about student loans – the cap and gown of debt types. They are a mix of good and potentially burdensome. On one hand, they're an investment in your future, but they can also be a heavy load to carry post-graduation. The key is to understand the terms and repayment options, making sure they align with your career trajectory and earning potential.

Consider the trendy but sneaky balloon loans – like that avant-garde piece that's exciting at first but can burden you with a substantial one-time payment at the end of the loan term. Opting for predictable loan structures can save you from a fashion faux pas in the future.

Lastly, there's consolidated debt – the capsule wardrobe that simplifies everything. If you're juggling multiple debt types, a consolidation loan can combine them into a single, manageable payment, often at a lower interest rate. It's like cleaning out your closet and keeping only what truly works for you.

Now that we've run our runway show of debt types, the takeaway is clear: understanding debt is all about context. What's essential is grasping the terms of each debt type, from interest rates to repayment schedules, and how they fit into your overall financial aesthetic. Borrow wisely, and you'll be accessorizing your financial future with savvy and grace.

Let's embrace this knowledge not as a burden but as liberation. With a clear understanding of the various types of debt, you're better equipped to make financial decisions that suit your lifestyle and goals. It's about creating a balance that lets you stride confidently towards financial independence in your chicest pair of heels, debt anxiety left far behind.

Remember, debt isn't inherently bad; it's about how you use it. Like the wardrobe choices you make, the financial decisions you make today shape your future image. Plan well, choose wisely, and your relationship with debt can be as comfortable and empowering as your favorite go-to outfit. Now, let's tackle those debts with the same gusto we go after the goals that spark joy and ambition in our lives.

Strategies for Paying Down Debt In the preceding chapters, we've dressed up our financial savvy and started strutting with confidence on the catwalk of monetary mindfulness. But what about the extra weight we've been carrying around — our debts? Just like any wardrobe mishap, debt can be managed with the right strategy.

Kicking off the high heels of denial, it's time for a sit-down with your debts. Let's start by listing them out - every credit card balance, student loan, car loan, and even that oh-so-generous loan from Aunt Linda. Seeing it all on paper can be tough, but it's the first step towards a debt-free catwalk.

Now, payment strategies aren't one-size-fits-all, but there are a few tried and true methods to paying down debt. The 'debt snowball' technique suggests starting with the smallest debt, regardless of interest rate, and making minimum payments on the rest. As each debt disappears, the payoff power moves to the next target. It's like knocking down dominoes - psychologically satisfying and motivating.

Alternatively, the 'debt avalanche' approach involves attacking the highest interest rate debts first. It's a methodical, number-crunching approach that saves you more in interest over time. Like preparing for a marathon, this method requires discipline and stamina, but the financial savings upon crossing the finish line can be significant.

For a more customized plan, consider the 'debt blizzard' — a mix of both snowball and avalanche. Pay off one small debt quickly for a quick motivational boost, then shift gears to high-interest debts, combining the psychological wins with savvy financial strategy.

Consider a balance transfer credit card for high-interest credit card debt. These cards often come with a 0% introductory interest rate, allowing you to make a dent in your principal without accruing interest for a set period. Do pay attention to balance transfer fees and the standard interest rate post-promotion, though, to avoid any unpleasant surprises.

Consolidating your debts can also streamline the repayment process. This involves taking out a new loan to pay off multiple debts, leaving you with a single payment. This can make your monthly outgoings more predictable and, if you secure a lower interest rate, reduce the amount you pay overall.

Consider also the power of extra payments. Even a little extra paid towards your debt each month can shave years and a significant amount of interest off your lifespan of debt. Small sacrifices now, like skipping that extra coffee or a night out, can have big payoffs later.

Leveraging technology can ease the burden too. There are apps and software designed to help you track and manage your debt repayments. They can help you visualize your progress, explore different repayment scenarios and automate your payments, so you never miss a due date.

Remember to reach out for help if you need it. Non-profit credit counseling agencies can offer guidance and even negotiate with lenders on your behalf for more manageable repayment terms or reduced interest rates.

But even with the best-laid plans, life happens. An emergency fund can prevent you from falling further into debt when unexpected expenses pop up. As much as paying down debt is a priority, don't neglect to put some money aside for those rainy days.

It's also essential to reflect on what led to the debt in the first place. Is it a matter of a one-time life event, or are there spending habits that need to change? Address the root of the issue to prevent debt from creeping back.

Avoid becoming overly frugal to the point of deprivation, though. Stripping your life of all joy can lead to burnout and a spending backlash. Instead, find a balance that allows for small indulgences while maintaining your debt repayment trajectory.

As you pay down each debt, celebrate your victories, no matter how small. Every step towards debt freedom deserves recognition. These celebrations need not be expensive; they are simply acknowledgments of your dedication and progress. Make it a ritual, as it will reinforce your commitment and keep you striding forward.

Lastly, always look forward. Once you achieve that thrilling zero balance, channel what you were paying into savings or investments. This shift not only safeguards you against future debt but also builds a foundation for wealth accumulation.

As you continue to implement these strategies, remember that paying down debt isn't just a financial act; it's an empowering journey towards financial independence. It's an investment in your future self, one where you exchange the heaviness of debt for the lightness of financial freedom. You're the leading lady of your own financial story – be bold, be persistent, and embrace the process with the courage of a woman who knows her worth.

Chapter 6:
Investing in Stilettos -
Introduction to Investing

Imagine a world where your wealth grows with as much grace and confidence as you carry yourself in your favorite pair of heels. That's the potential power of investing, where seizing smart opportunities can elevate both your stature and your bank balance. This chapter is an open doorway to the vibrant ballroom of investing—a place where jargon turns into juicy possibilities, and where terms like stocks and bonds begin to tangle with your personal goals, setting the rhythm for financial success. Think of this as the pre-party, and what a warm-up we've got! We're laying down the red carpet, clearing up the mystique around the market, and ensuring you can navigate the nitty-gritty of investment options with the poise of a pro. After all, your money deserves to dance to a rhythm that resonates with your ambitions and dreams. It's time to step up to the challenge; let's unleash the savvy investor in you and orchestrate a portfolio that harmonizes perfectly with your future plans.

Investment 101: Terms and Strategies Inherently, investing might seem like a territory dominated by stiff suits and complex jargon, but strip it back to the basics and what you have is a powerful tool for wealth creation, even in heels! Let's step into the world where terms like "assets" and "dividends" become part of your lexicon, and strategies like "diversification" and "asset allocation" frame the canvas of your financial masterpiece. Ready?

First, let's define an *asset*. It's anything you own that can provide future economic benefit. That includes stocks, bonds, property, even your handbag collection if it appreciates over time! Now, unlike that stunning pair of Louboutins, *stocks* represent ownership in a company. When you buy a stock, you're banking on the company growing over time, and as it does, so does the value of your share.

Bonds, on the other side of the heel, are akin to lending money. You're playing it safer, usually with lower returns, compared to stocks. Governments or corporations borrow your money and pay you back with interest over an agreed period—rather like an IOU with benefits.

But how can you earn from these assets? Enter *dividends*, a company's way of sharing profits with shareholders. It's essentially getting paid to hold onto those shares. Dividends can provide a steady stream of income without having to sell your stocks, which can be pretty fabulous if you ask me.

However, one company's downfall shouldn't be your financial undoing. That's where *diversification* struts in. It involves spreading investments across various asset classes or sectors to minimize risks. Think of it as not putting all your eggs in one designer handbag.

Understanding *risk tolerance* is vital as well. It's all about how much volatility you can stomach. If the thought of sharp drops in your investment value has you reaching for a paper bag, you might prefer a conservative approach with lower-risk assets like bonds or money market funds.

Asset allocation is like organizing your closet. It's the process of deciding where to put your investment money based on personal goals, risk tolerance, and time horizon. Determining the right mix of stocks, bonds, and other assets is crucial for optimized portfolio performance.

A term that often trips up beginners is *market capitalization*, or market cap for short. It's what you get when you multiply a company's share price by the total number of shares. Why care? Because companies are grouped by size — large-cap, mid-cap, and small-cap, and each has distinct characteristics and associated risks.

Let's touch on *indexes*, which are like benchmarks for measuring how a portion of the market is performing. Ever heard of the S&P 500 or the Dow Jones? These indexes help you understand market trends and how well your own investments stack up against them.

The strategy you choose should sync with your goals. Are you saving for a downpayment on a chic loft, or are you building a nest egg for decades from now? Short-term investors might prefer *value investing*, hunting for undervalued stocks to sell when the market corrects. Long-term investors often lean towards *growth investing*, choosing companies with potential for significant earnings growth.

Another head-turner is *mutual funds*. These bundle together a mix of investments, managed by professionals who chase the goals of the fund. It's a way to achieve diversification without having to individually pick every stock or bond yourself.

Of course, none of this comes without *fees and taxes*. Understanding the costs associated with investing, from fund management fees to capital gains tax, is crucial. The less you pay for these, the more of your money starts working for you.

Automation has become a chic investor's best friend. Consider setting up *automatic contributions* to your investment accounts. It's like putting your savings on autopilot—all in favor of that growing investment wardrobe.

Now, amidst all this, don't underestimate the power of *patience*. Investments aren't about instant gratification. The market has moods, darlings. It swings. It dips. It soars. Having the resilience to ride these ups and downs can be as crucial as choosing the right investments themselves.

Lastly, keep an open mind towards continued learning. Investment landscapes change, and what works today may need tweaking tomorrow. Stay informed, stay nimble, and always, always keep your investment strategy in sync with your personal goals.

In essence, the world of investing is less daunting when you're equipped with the right terms and strategies. Remember, you're not just saving money; you're building an empire, one investment at a time. Empowerment comes from knowledge and action—so let's make those money moves with confidence, grace, and a touch of glamour.

Types of Investments: Stocks, Bonds, and More Ladies, let's talk about growing your money garden with an assortment of investment flowers like stocks, bonds, and other investment vehicles that can add color and contrast to your financial picture. Imagine a portfolio as your personal financial garden — you want it diverse and blooming all year round, right? Diversification is key, not just for aesthetics but for robustness through the seasons of the economy.

Starting with stocks, they're like the sun-loving perennials that can grow strong with enough light. When you buy stock, you're buying a small piece of a company. If the company does well, your shares could increase in value, and you might receive dividends as your share of the profits. Remember, the stock market can be volatile, so prices can fluctuate wildly, but for those with a long-term view and a taste for growth, stocks have historically outperformed many other investments.

Bonds, on the other hand, are the evergreens providing consistent, reliable color even when the garden is dormant. They are loans you give to governments or corporations, and in return, they pay you interest over a set period. It's typically a less risky investment than stocks, offering a fixed income stream, though with interest rates fluctuating, the value of bonds can go up or down.

Short of being the sole lover of stocks or strictly a bond enthusiast, mutual funds are like a ready-made mixed border. They pool money from many investors to buy a diversified mixture of stocks and/or bonds. They offer instant diversification and are managed by professionals, which can be a great relief if you don't have the time or desire to manage individual investments.

Exchange-traded funds (ETFs), like striking accent pieces, offer even more flexibility. Like mutual funds, ETFs hold a variety of investments, but they trade on an exchange like a stock. This means you can buy and sell ETFs throughout the trading day, and they often come with lower fees than mutual funds.

Index funds are akin to planting a swath of wildflowers, where the mix naturally reflects the diversity of the field (or in this case, a market index). These funds aim to match the performance of a specific index, such as the S&P 500, by holding the same stocks in the same proportions as the index. They're a low-cost and passive strategy, as they don't require active management.

If the idea of an investment that offers support in turbulent times appeals to you, consider the stability of high-yield savings accounts and certificates of deposit (CDs). They're like the hardscaping in your garden, less likely to be swayed by the weather and offering a steady visual anchor. These are insured by the FDIC, which means they offer a risk-free return, albeit typically smaller than what you might get from riskier investments.

Real estate investments can be the statuesque trees that take a while to mature but offer substantial value and presence once they do. Whether you're buying property directly or investing in real estate investment trusts (REITs), real estate can offer potential for appreciation in value, rental income, and tax advantages.

Commodities like gold or oil can be likened to exotic plants — they can add rarity and a hedge against inflation, but they can also be more volatile. These are physical goods that can be a great way to diversify your investment garden and shield it against the ups and downs of the stock market.

Let's not forget about the newer saplings in the garden — cryptocurrencies. They are the wildflowers that can be unpredictable and may not grow where you want them to. They're digital assets using blockchain technology, offering potential high rewards but also carrying substantial risk. If you're going to allocate part of your garden to these, make sure it's an amount you're willing to experiment with.

The beauty of your financial garden is that it's uniquely yours. It should align with your financial goals, whether you're building a flashy show garden or a serene retreat. Understanding the different types of investments allows you to choose what best fits your temperament, your stage in life, and your long-term objectives.

Note that this list is not exhaustive, and there are more nuanced investment vehicles available, such as options, annuities, and private equity. Each comes with its own set of care instructions and growth patterns, so it's essential to educate yourself or consult a financial advisor to understand the risks and benefits thoroughly.

Remember, investing isn't just about making money—it's about making your money work for you, creating a financial buffer against uncertainties, and allowing you the freedom to live your life on your terms. Like any skilled gardener knows, patience, knowledge, and attentiveness can lead to a thriving and beautiful landscape. Nurture your investments with care and they will bloom wonderfully over time.

Empowerment starts with knowledge, and by familiarizing yourself with the vast world of investments, you're setting the stage for a rich and rewarding financial future. Keep watering and tending to your garden, and rest assured that with each decision, you become more rooted in your journey toward financial independence.

Now that you have an overview of the types of investments that can adorn your financial garden, we'll move on to the art of crafting your personal investment portfolio. This will be your blueprint for which flowers, shrubs, trees, and ornamental features you'll plant to create harmony and balance while aligning with your financial aspirations.

Crafting Your Investment Portfolio Imagine strutting into your financial future with confidence, heels clicking with every step. That's the kind of assurance we're aiming for as you craft your investment portfolio. It's more than just picking stocks or tossing money into a fund; it's about creating a masterpiece that reflects your goals, your values, and yes, your style. So let's discuss how to curate an investment collection as unique and powerful as you are.

The first step in crafting your portfolio is understanding your timeline. Are you investing with a view of cashing out soon, maybe for a down payment on a house? Or are you looking ahead to the distant horizon of retirement? Your timeline influences the types of investments you'll choose. For shorter terms, you might opt for more liquid and less volatile investments. For the long haul, you're in a position to ride out the market's ups and downs for potentially greater returns.

Next, let's talk risk tolerance. It's like picking out a new perfume – you have to find the scent that feels right. Some investments have the potential for high returns but come with the risk of high losses. Others are as steady as a classic scent, with smaller, but more predictable outcomes. Be honest with yourself. If the thought of market dips sends you into a panic, a conservative approach might be for you. If you're comfortable riding the investment roller coaster, a bolder strategy could suit your style.

Now, onto the fun part – diversification. This is the little black dress of investing. It never goes out of style and it's essential for every occasion. Diversification is about spreading your investments across different asset classes like stocks, bonds, and real estate, or within them, like various sectors and industries. This way, if one investment falters, another might flourish, balancing your risk.

As you select your investments, think about costs. Fees can eat into your returns much like how shipping fees can take the joy out of online shopping. Look for low-fee index funds or ETFs. And when you work with financial professionals, understand how they're compensated. A fee-based advisor who charges for advice regardless of the products they sell can be more aligned with your best interests.

Strategic asset allocation is your blueprint. This is a fancy term for deciding what portion of your portfolio you want in stocks, bonds, and other assets, and it should reflect your risk tolerance and timeline. It's not static either; you'll want to revisit and adjust as you stride through different life stages.

Monitoring your portfolio is like checking in on your favorite social media feeds – do it regularly, but don't obsess. The markets will have their fluctuations and it's best to think long term. Keep an eye out for significant life changes or a shift in your goals, though. These events might prompt some tweaks to your portfolio.

When you're ready to invest, consider starting small and automating your investments. Think of it as setting up a subscription box for your financial future; money is invested before you can even think about spending it. Over time, these automatic contributions can really add up, thanks to the magic of compounding interest.

Remember, you're not in this alone. There's a wealth of resources out there from books to podcasts to online communities where you can learn and grow. Don't be shy to seek out a financial advisor either. It's like having a personal trainer for your bank account.

Let's get personal for a moment. Your values matter, and impact investing allows you to put your money where your heart is. Want to support women-led businesses? There are funds for that. Passionate about environmental sustainability? Green investments are calling your name. Aligning your portfolio with your principles is not only fulfilling, but it can also influence positive change.

Adjustment and adaptation are key. Reinventing your portfolio over time is as normal as switching up your wardrobe for a new season. Economic climates change, industries evolve, and new opportunities emerge. Keeping your investment strategy flexible will ensure your portfolio stays fresh and functional.

Tax efficiency might not be the most thrilling topic, but it's important. Be savvy about the potential tax implications of your investments. Things like tax-loss harvesting and the right account types can make a real difference in your after-tax returns, which is what really counts.

And let's not forget about the rest of your financial plan. Your investment portfolio isn't a standalone accessory; it's part of an entire ensemble. Ensure it complements your emergency fund, insurance coverage, and debts. Think of your portfolio as part of a cohesive look that works together to make you financially fabulous.

Lastly, stay educated. Markets and financial products are constantly evolving. Keep up with the latest trends and continue learning. You wouldn't wear last season's trends this year, so don't let your portfolio get outdated either.

Your investment portfolio is your ticket to financial independence. It's your hard-earned money working for you, allowing you the freedom to live life on your terms. So invest with focus, invest with style, and watch as your portfolio becomes a powerful testament to your financial savvy and independence.

Carving out your financial niche in this world is an exciting journey, and crafting your investment portfolio with care is a vital part of that adventure. Through wise investment choices and a strategic mindset, you're setting the stage for a prosperous and empowered future. You've got the drive, the smarts, and the savoir-faire—now go forth and invest with the same confidence and elegance that you bring to every other aspect of your life.

Risk vs. Reward: Finding Your Comfort Zone As we lace up our financial stilettos and step into the world of investing, it becomes urgently crucial to understand the balance between risk and reward. This delicate dance can either propel us to the pinnacle of fiscal empowerment or leave us nursing the blisters of disappointment. It's about finding that sweet spot – a comfort zone where the excitement of potential gains doesn't keep us awake at night with worry.

Finding your comfort zone in investing doesn't mean you shy away from all risk. After all, every great success story includes chapters where the protagonists take calculated risks. What's important is aligning your investments with your personal risk tolerance and financial goals. Like finding the perfect dress – it's not just about the look but also about the fit and feel.

The stunning thing about investing is that it's not one-size-fits-all. Your best friend might be all about those high heeled, high-risk stocks, living for the adrenaline of the market's ups and downs. But maybe you? You prefer the ballet flats of bonds, the steady and stylish choice providing grounding and less chance for a stumble. That's totally fine!

To find your comfort zone, first acknowledge your current financial situation and life stage. Are you a young professional with years ahead to recover from potential market dips? Or maybe you're edging closer to retirement and seeking more security in your investments? Your timeline significantly influences how much risk you can comfortably take on.

Next up: understanding yourself. Just like knowing your true shoe size instead of squeezing into an ill-fitting pair, it's critical to take a step back and assess your own risk tolerance. Are you the kind of person who's kept up at night by the slightest fluctuation in your investments? Or can you keep a cool head, trusting in the process over the long term? The answers to these questions help tailor your investment strategy to suit your sleep-well-at-night level.

But it's not just about comfort. It's also about growth. It might mean stepping out of your comfort zone now and then to achieve a more rewarding future. Just like investing in a high-quality handbag that'll stand the test of time, sometimes going for a slightly bolder investment can pay off in the long run.

It's also essential to talk about diversification – it's like the wardrobe of your investment strategy. You wouldn't wear the same outfit every day, so why would you put all your financial eggs in one basket? Spreading your investments across different assets can help manage risk while still giving you access to the rewards of different markets and sectors.

Consider speaking with a financial advisor; it's sort of like consulting a personal stylist for your finances. They can provide personalized advice that fits your unique financial situation and goals, helping you navigate the vast world of investing without feeling overwhelmed.

And let's not forget about education. The more you know, the better decisions you'll make. You wouldn't buy a car without understanding its features; the same goes for investments. Understanding the basics of stocks, bonds, ETFs, and other investment vehicles becomes your roadmap for navigating the avenues of the financial world.

Another essential strategy is to set boundaries. Determine in advance how much of a drop in investment value you can tolerate before you feel compelled to sell. This strategy, akin to deciding when to leave a party, helps prevent emotion-driven decisions that could hurt your financial well-being.

Remember, volatility in the market is normal, much like the season's trends in fashion. A savvy investor understands that short-term fluctuations shouldn't distract from long-term financial goals. Keep your eyes on the horizon, where the rewards often wait for those who are patient.

Also, don't be afraid to reevaluate and adjust your strategy. Just as you might outgrow a style or find a new love for a different type of heel, your investment comfort zone can change. Life events such as a new job, marriage, or a growing family can all warrant a fresh look at your investment approach.

While we're at it, let's debunk a myth: more risk doesn't always mean more reward. Sometimes the best rewards come from consistent, measured steps – think compound interest from a stable, if not particularly glamorous, investment. It's about finding the right opportunities that align with your appetite for risk.

Don't forget to celebrate victories along the way. Perhaps you've hit a personal savings milestone or your investment has grown by a certain percentage. Acknowledging these triumphs is not only satisfying but can also motivate you to continue making wise financial decisions.

In conclusion, finding your comfort zone in the realm of risk versus reward is a personal journey. It's critical to balance a desire for growth with the need for a good night's rest. By understanding your financial landscape, acknowledging your personal risk tolerance, and staying educated and diversified, you can strut confidently through the stock market runway. Be patient, be persistent, and let your investments reflect not only your financial ambitions but your unique lifestyle and personality as well.

Chapter 7:
Real Estate and Rosé -
Property Investment for Women

As we uncork the robust world of property investment, it's time to pour ourselves a glass of empowerment and taste the freedom that real estate can offer. Diving into this shimmering pool isn't just for the suited moguls you might picture; it's a territory where today's savvy woman can thrive. Property investment is the ultimate asset class that combines solid bricks-and-mortar security with the potential for delightful returns—much like a well-chosen bottle of rosé. However, getting in on the real estate game isn't merely about snatching up any old property. It's about strategic choices, understanding market trends, and knowing when to hold onto your investment for the long haul or flip it for quick gains. And guess what? It's not just about having enough cash; it's about equipping yourself with the right tools and confidence to take on this traditionally male-dominated field. Deepen your pockets through property, untoasted hint of passive income, and watch as your financial portfolio blooms with a stability and vibrancy that mirrors your own inner strength. In this chapter, let's demystify the real estate jargon and uncover the sparkling truth that women can, and should, make a splash in property investment.

The Basics of Real Estate Investment Real estate investment might sound like the realm of the rich and experienced, but let's shatter that glass ceiling, shall we? Imagine turning the key to not just a home, but an investment that works for you. The beauty of real estate is its tangible nature - you can touch it, you can enhance it, and you can use it to generate income. Whether you're envisioning a cozy bungalow or a chic apartment building, the basics are the same. So, let's start setting those foundation stones.

First things first, real estate investment doesn't require a fortune to begin. You might start with purchasing a small rental property. The most traditional path is buying a property and renting it out to cover the mortgage and hopefully, bring in a little extra on the side. It's a thrilling thought, right? Being a landlord, having tenants, and collecting rent could be your next empowerment move.

Another basic concept in real estate is 'appreciation'. This is the increase in the value of your property over time. While markets fluctuate, in the long run, real estate typically appreciates. This can lead to significant gains when you decide to sell. And let's not forget about leverage. Using borrowed capital for the acquisition of an asset could amplify your potential return - a strategic way to take larger strides in the investment world.

Let's talk location because, in real estate, it's everything. Choosing the right neighborhood, understanding community plans, and studying market trends are critical. A developing area might offer growth potential, but established neighborhoods could provide stability. Think of yourself as a visionary, seeking out areas that whisper 'future hotspot' rather than those that shout 'peak prices'.

Investing in residential properties is one way to sip the real estate cocktail, but commercial properties can also be enticing. Imagine owning a small boutique shop filled with vibrant clientes or an office space where ideas bloom. These properties typically involve longer leases and might offer better rental yields, although they can also require more upfront investment.

Now, being a property owner calls for strategy and management. You have to become adept at balancing the books, from managing maintenance costs to understanding property taxes. Jargon like 'cash flow' and 'capital expenditures' becomes part of your vocabulary. Positive cash flow – when the rental income exceeds all expenses – is music to an investor's ears.

Financing your foray into property investment may involve mortgages, which are loans specifically for real estate. Shopping around for the best mortgage rates and terms that suit your goals is like hunting for that perfect pair of shoes - it takes patience, but when you find the right fit, you move with confidence.

Your investment property can also serve as a tax shield. Yes, you read that right. You can often deduct mortgage interest, operating expenses, and even depreciation from your taxes. Consult with a tax professional to navigate these waters, as they could substantially improve your investment's performance.

But wait, there's more. 'Real Estate Investment Trusts (REITs)' offer a way to dip your toes into the real estate market without buying physical property. These companies own and manage real estate portfolios, and you can invest in them much like you would with stocks. A great way to be part of the real estate dance floor, even with a smaller purse.

Some investors prefer 'house flipping,' buying undervalued properties, renovating them, and selling for profit. It's like giving a house a makeover and sending it out into the world anew. It can be a quick way to make money, but be warned, it's not as easy as reality TV makes it look; it can be risky and demands market savvy.

Of course, let's not overlook 'risk management'. Knowing how much you can afford to invest and how much risk you can handle is key. Can you weather vacancies or unexpected repairs? Knowing your limits can help prevent financial overextension. After all, real estate is a powerful investment vehicle, but it shouldn't drive you off a cliff.

Networking is also part of the basics. Real estate is often about who you know, as well as what you know. Linking up with other investors, joining real estate clubs, attending seminars, or even following online forums can provide invaluable insights and opportunities.

In your journey to real estate investing, remember that your mindset is your most valued asset. Stay curious, learn continuously, and don't be afraid to ask questions. The field constantly evolves, and staying informed puts you in a position to seize opportunities when they arise.

Real estate may seem daunting at first, but emphasizing education, strategy, and patience turns it into an empowering endeavor. Start by immersing yourself in the basics right now, and soon you might see your financial portrait painted with the broad strokes of property ownership and investment. As with any masterpiece, it begins with a single brushstroke – or in this case, a single property.

To wrap up, the basics of real estate investment are much like learning to walk in high heels. There may be some wobbles and uncertainty at first, but with practice and confidence, you're poised to strut into a world of opportunities. With a clear understanding of real estate principles, you open doors not just to physical properties, but to potential wealth and financial independence – goals worthy of any ambitious woman's aspirations.

Generating Passive Income Through Property Transitioning gracefully from the world of high-heels and high finance, let's shift our focus towards bricks and mortar. Have you ever dreamt of lounging on your couch sipping a glass of rosé while your bank account continues to grow? It's not a fantasy, and with some savvy moves, property investment could be your ticket to passive income.

First off, let's demystify the concept of passive income. It's money that flows in regularly without requiring constant hands-on work. In the realm of property, this usually means either rental income from tenants or gains from property value increases over time. Now, let's think long-term – passive doesn't mean effort-free. Establishing a stream of income through real estate necessitates an upfront commitment of time, energy, and, indeed, capital.

Starting on the right foot means picking the right property. It's about more than just falling in love with a charming little house or a chic apartment. Delve deeply into the numbers and forecast your potential return on investment. And remember, location, location, location! It's not just a cliché – the charm of an area, accessibility to amenities, and potential for growth can seriously affect your earnings. Don't forget to keep your eyes open for emerging neighborhoods that promise future value spikes.

Are you worried about the down payment? You might be pleasantly surprised at the number of creative financing options out there. From traditional mortgages to real estate investment groups, you can find a solution tailored to your financial situation. Be diligent in exploring these options but also cautious not to overextend yourself. In real estate, sustainable leverage is key.

Renting out property can be a gold mine or a money pit, and discernment is your best friend in avoiding the latter. Finding trustworthy tenants takes patience but it's critical. Consider hiring a property management company if screening tenants and responding to late-night leaky faucet calls isn't your cup of tea. Yes, it's an extra expense, but weigh it against the time and energy you'll save.

Now, let's dive into the tax benefits. Thanks to deductions on mortgage interest, property taxes, operating expenses, and depreciation, owning rental property can trim down your tax bill. Consult with a savvy tax advisor who can guide you through maximizing these benefits. Remember that tax laws can be complex, so expert advice is crucial to ensure you're compliant while also strategically reducing your tax liabilities.

If hands-on management isn't for you, consider real estate investment trusts (REITs). They're companies that own income-producing real estate and offer investors a way to invest in portfolios of properties without owning them directly. You can buy shares in REITs just like stocks, enjoying dividends, and without the nitty-gritty of property management.

Leveraging can also mean pooling resources with partners or investors to get your foot in the property door. This can lower individual risk and allow you to invest in larger properties that you couldn't afford alone. But like any relationship, choose partners with care and have clear agreements to keep misunderstandings at bay.

Thinking of flipping houses to generate income? It can be fulfilling, but it's not for the faint-hearted. Flipping involves buying properties, renovating them, and selling for profit. You'll need a solid understanding of the real estate market and renovation costs to make it profitable. Additionally, adopt a strategic approach to upgrades, focusing on changes that offer the best return on investment.

For the more adventurous investors, vacation rentals offer another avenue. Platforms like Airbnb have popularized short-term rentals, and they can be more profitable than long-term ones. However, the market can be seasonal and management more hands-on. This approach suits those with a knack for hospitality and marketing – turning a property into a desirable vacation spot can lead to an excellent revenue stream.

Let's not gloss over the risks – while the rewards can be high, so can the potential pitfalls. Unforeseen maintenance, problematic tenants, market downturns, and regulatory changes can turn your investment sour. Diversification is your safety net, so don't put all your eggs in one real estate basket.

Investing in property also requires a forward-thinking mindset. The market might not be ripe for selling when you plan to exit your investment. Flexibility, patience, and a keen eye on market trends are paramount. It's not just about earning rent – it's about capital growth over time, which can significantly affect the success of your investment.

Education is your ally. Read voraciously, join investment communities, attend workshops, and maybe even find a mentor. A well-informed investor is one poised for success. Keep abreast of the latest market trends, legal requirements, and best practices. Information can be the difference between a profitable investment and a costly mistake.

Being a female investor in the property game can be empowering. Prove the stereotype wrong – you are as financially astute and investment-savvy as anyone else with the added benefit of intuition and a unique perspective. Use these to your advantage, recognize good opportunities, and don't hesitate to negotiate hard for them. Involve yourself in a network of like-minded women where you can share insights and support each other's property aspirations.

Let's wrap this up with a regular reminder to reflect on your financial goals. Every property purchase or investment should be aligned with where you want to be in the future. Think of it as building not just a portfolio, but a legacy. Let your investments pave the way for financial freedom, where passive income allows you to live the life you've always imagined.

Finally, remember that wealth-building takes time. Property investment may be a slow burner, but when done thoughtfully, it can be utterly transformative. Set the foundation now with strategic choices, and watch as your financial landscape flourishes, reaping the benefits in the form of that beautiful, flowing, passive income.

Chapter 8:
401(k)s, IRAs, and ETFs -
Navigating Retirement Accounts

As we pivot from the brick-and-mortar world of real estate investing, let's shift gears to the backbone of your golden years - retirement accounts. It's time to dive into the alphabet soup of 401(k)s, IRAs, and ETFs, and I promise it's not as daunting as it seems. Think of these accounts as your future self's best friends. A 401(k) isn't just a number before the alphabet's coolest letter; it's a powerful tool that, with employer match, can feel like a work bonus that keeps on giving. IRAs, both traditional and Roth, offer amazing tax advantages that can help you maximize your savings. And don't overlook ETFs – these versatile funds can be vital players in both your retirement accounts and your broader investment strategy. In this chapter, we'll untangle the often confusing aspects of these accounts, talk about how to make them work for you, and how to turn them into your retirement runway. So let's get savvy about stashing that cash and ensure that when retirement comes knocking, you're ready to answer with confidence and style.

Understanding Your Retirement Options Transitioning into our talk on retirement, it's not just about kicking up your heels and sipping margaritas on the beach—although, let's be honest, that image does have its appeal. It's about grappling with a multitude of paths and vehicles that can get you to that restful shoreline. Taking control of your future means understanding the nitty-gritty of retirement options, regardless of whether you're a young professional just starting out, an entrepreneur facing a slew of investment decisions, or nearing the end of a career and eyeing that horizon.

The traditional option many think of first is the tried-and-true 401(k). Offered by many employers, it allows for pre-tax contributions—which reduce your taxable income—while providing a possible company match. Yes, it's like getting free money for your golden years. Ladies, always aim to max out that match; it's an invaluable part of your compensation package.

For the self-employed or those without an employer-sponsored plan, an IRA, or Individual Retirement Account, steps into the spotlight. Whether you opt for a Traditional IRA with its tax-deferred growth potential or a Roth IRA with tax-free withdrawals in retirement, each has its own dance card of benefits.

Let's also not overlook the SEP-IRA, a darling among entrepreneurs and self-employed mavens. With higher contribution limits, it's a robust vehicle for those with higher incomes looking to shelter more money from taxes.

Now, you might've heard of the mystical unicorn known as the pension plan. It's becoming increasingly rare, but some sectors—like government and education—still offer these defined benefit plans. If you have access to this majestic creature, understand the terms and conditions, because they're usually designed to provide a set income in retirement.

Diving deeper, there's the alluring world of annuities. These financial instruments can offer a steady income stream in retirement and come in various flavors—immediate, fixed, variable, indexed. Weigh the costs and benefits, because while the promise of guaranteed income is tempting, annuities can be complex and require diligent consideration.

If you're feeling socially savvy and have eagle-eyed focus, consider the solo 401(k). It's tailored for business owners with no employees, allowing them to wear the dual hats of employer and employee, hence doubling their contribution potential. It's a versatile choice for those who relish flexibility and control.

Don't forget about diversification—it's your financial wardrobe's best friend. While planning for retirement, keep a mix of investments, like stocks, bonds, mutual funds, and perhaps real estate, within these retirement accounts to spread out and manage risk.

And let's talk about portability for a second. Life is a journey full of transitions, and your retirement plan should have the ability to roll with the punches. Whether you leave a job, change careers, or start your own business, understanding the process of rolling over your retirement funds to prevent penalties and maintain tax benefits is crucial.

It's also worth peeking at the horizon of new retirement options. Things like health savings accounts (HSAs) which—believe it or not—can double as a retirement savings vehicle due to their threefold tax advantage. Or exploring catch-up contributions, the financial equivalent of a power move for those over age 50 who need to bolster their savings.

Understanding your retirement options also involves a good grip on Social Security benefits. It's like the baseline rhythm to your retirement melody. Knowing how much you can expect to receive, and the optimal age to start taking benefits, is vital to your long-term financial symphony. Don't leave it to fate—understanding your projected benefits early on can inform better decisions about your overall retirement timing and strategy.

For the globally-minded among us, remember that your retirement accounts and strategies don't have to be confined within the borders of the United States. It's possible to hold certain international investments within these accounts, just be sure to understand the rules and implications.

Lastly, we must address the psychological transition into retirement. It's more than just financial readiness; it's preparing your heart and mind for a significant lifestyle shift. Start envisioning what your ideal retirement looks like now and build a financial plan that leads you there gracefully.

In this wealth of retirement options, there's beauty in the variety and power in choice. Start by taking inventory of which retirement instruments resonate with your financial tune. Sit down with a financial professional if you need to—even powerhouses need a sounding board from time to time.

Take these insights and weave them into your larger financial fabric. Your future self—perhaps sporting a fabulous wide-brim hat on that sunny beach—will thank you for the diligent planning and savvy decisions you made. Embrace the journey, and know that every smart choice you make today is a step towards a lifetime of independence and style.

Maximizing Employer Benefits and Contributions Transitioning from discussing the variety of retirement accounts available, it's vital to zoom in on a crucial aspect - maximizing your benefits from the ones sponsored by your employer. Let me walk you through a strategy session on leveraging these benefits to bolster your financial foundation.

First off, if your employer offers a 401(k) or similar retirement plan with a matching contribution, prioritize contributing enough to get the full match. Why leave free money on the table? A common match might be 50% of your contributions up to 6% of your salary. By not contributing at least that 6%, you're essentially turning down a raise.

Dig into the details of your benefits package. Beyond basic contributions, there may be profit-sharing plans or stock options. Take advantage of these offers when they align with your financial goals. Stock options, especially, can be powerful tools when used wisely, allowing you to share in the company's potential success.

Understanding vesting schedules is also vital. Some companies require that you work a certain number of years before their contributions to your retirement account fully belong to you. Plan your career moves accordingly to ensure you don't lose out on these accumulated assets.

Consider the advantages of a Health Savings Account (HSA) if your employer offers it alongside a high-deductible health plan. An HSA is not just for medical expenses; it's a stealth retirement account with triple tax benefits - contributions are tax-deductible, the balance grows tax-free, and withdrawals are untaxed when used for qualified medical expenses.

Don't ignore Flexible Spending Accounts (FSAs) either. Like HSAs, FSAs have tax benefits for healthcare costs but be wary of the use-it-or-lose-it rule. Plan your contributions based on anticipated medical expenses so that you maximize the benefit without wasting funds.

When it comes to pensions, if you're lucky enough to have a defined-benefit plan, understand the formula for benefit calculations. Your pension could be a substantial part of your retirement income, so consider how your working years and salary progression impact your future payments.

Look for other perks that can indirectly boost your financial health. Discounts on services and products, education assistance, and wellness programs are more than mere perks; they're opportunities for savings. These benefits can reduce your out-of-pocket expenses and can be redirected to saving or investing.

Be aware of life and disability insurance options through your employer. Often, you can acquire this coverage at a group rate, which is typically lower than what you'd find on the open market. Having the right insurance coverage is just as much a part of your financial plan as saving for retirement.

Don't be passive about your benefits. Review your benefits package at least annually, as companies can change providers, benefits, or their contributions. Staying informed ensures you're always making the best decisions with the latest information.

If you're ever in doubt about your benefits, don't hesitate to contact your HR department or a benefits counselor. They are there to help and can provide clarity on complex topics like deferred compensation plans or special executive-level benefits.

For those eyeing a job change, benefits should play a significant role in your decision-making. A new role might come with a raise, but if their benefits package is less generous, you might find yourself at a financial loss in the long run. Consider the total compensation package, not just the salary.

If you're in the entrepreneurial realm, maximizing employer benefits shifts to creating your own. If you run your own business, look into establishing a retirement plan like a SEP IRA or Solo 401(k) where you can make substantial contributions to your retirement savings.

Finally, when it comes to employer benefits, don't operate in a silo. Network with colleagues to understand how they're maximizing their benefits. Sometimes, the most innovative strategies come from a casual conversation during a coffee break.

Remember, navigating your employer's benefits landscape is not just a one-time activity; it's an ongoing process that requires attention and action. By maximizing these benefits, you're not only enhancing your current financial well-being but also fortifying your road to financial independence.

Commit to becoming the CFO of your personal finances and view each benefit as a tool to grow your wealth. Treat your employer's benefits as critical components of your overall investment strategy—a strategy wherein you're always looking for the next smart move to get you closer to that picture of financial independence dancing in your head.

So, take charge and maximize every contribution, benefit, and opportunity afforded to you through your work. These are the stepping stones on your path to securing a robust financial future—one where you call the shots with confidence, elegance, and uncompromising savvy.

Chapter 9:
Wall Street Wisdom -
Stock Market Basics

Ladies, imagine Wall Street as the ultimate shopping district where instead of window-shopping, you're acquiring pieces of companies that can grow in value over time. Welcome to the stock market, the bustling epicenter of commerce where bits of paper, or now digital entries, represent ownership in corporations and present opportunities for wealth expansion. Understanding how the stock market functions is like learning a new language—one that speaks in ticks, trades, and trajectories. It's the backbone of investment portfolios, where diversification is the stylish accessory you simply can't ignore. Here, we demystify what can often seem like an alphabet soup of acronyms and jargon, laying out a foundational understanding that empowers you to engage with confidence. We'll navigate through the essential concepts you'll need, ensuring you walk away not just with theoretical knowledge, but with practical wisdom that prepares you for the next steps in building a resilient and diversified investment portfolio. So, let's roll up our sleeves and get to the heart of what makes the stock market tick—it's not just for the pinstriped suits anymore; it's a place where your financial independence takes center stage.

How the Stock Market Works – this may seem like a topic shrouded in mystery, but it's essential understanding material for anyone aiming to craft a confident financial future. The stock market is the thriving heart of the financial world – a dynamic marketplace where ownership of businesses changes hands from minute to minute. It can be your avenue to financial empowerment, and with a solid grasp of its mechanics, you stand to unlock opportunities that can contribute significantly to your wealth-building journey.

In essence, the stock market is a public sphere that allows buyers and sellers to transact in stock shares – pieces of ownership in a company. When you buy a stock, you're not just purchasing a slip of paper or a digital entry; you're acquiring a portion of that company and, by extension, a share in its success or failure. Over time, the aim is that these businesses grow and become more valuable, increasing the value of your shares and your overall wealth.

Stock exchanges, like the New York Stock Exchange or the NASDAQ, provide the platforms where this all plays out. Think of them as bustling farmers' markets, but instead of fruit and veggies, it's shares that are up for grabs. Companies must meet specific requirements to list their stocks on an exchange – a process known as an Initial Public Offering (IPO), which itself is an event many investors watch closely as it can offer lucrative opportunities.

The prices of stocks are influenced by a myriad of factors encompassing company performance, economic conditions, and global events – down to the more psychological aspects of how investors feel about a company's future prospects. This constant ebb and flow of price is the market's beating pulse, and it's where the savvy investor, armed with research and insight, can thrive.

Operating like a complex yet attainable game, the stock market functions through a system of supply and demand. If a particular stock is the darling of the day, with more people wanting to buy it than sell it, the price typically goes up. Conversely, if the world is sour on a stock and shares flood the market with few buyers, the price generally takes a tumble.

The stock market also plays a crucial role in helping companies themselves. By selling shares, they can raise capital without incurring debt. This money can springboard growth opportunities like research, development, and expansion – elements critical for both the company's evolution and your potential profit as a shareholder.

As investors, we interact with the stock market through brokers – think of them as your guides or intermediaries. Today, it's often done electronically with a swipe or a click, but behind the scenes, it's all about matching buyers and sellers in the most efficient and equitable way possible. Modern technology has democratized access to the stock market, making it so that you can start building your portfolio at virtually any point, with whatever means you can sensibly invest.

Investing in the stock market comes with its risks – there's no denying that. It's vital to recognize that stocks can lose value, sometimes precipitously. However, there's an undeniable trend that over the long term, the stock market has grown. That's why it's crucial not only to dive in but to persist, to pay attention, and to build a portfolio aligned with your financial goals and risk tolerance.

When it comes to stock markets, the term 'diversification' is your knight in shining armor. It means not putting all your eggs in one basket but spreading your investments across different sectors, industries, and even countries. This way, if one investment dips, you're not left high and dry; others in your portfolio can offer a counterbalance.

Understanding the psychological highs and lows of the market is crucial too. The market can be swayed significantly by investor sentiment, often causing people to act impulsively. A calm and researched approach, looking beyond short-term fluctuations, is what separates the novices from the masters of this realm.

Indices or indexes like the Dow Jones Industrial Average and the S&P 500 track groups of stocks, offering a snapshot of the market's overall health. These benchmarks are often referenced in news reports and can serve as a gauge for how well your investments are performing in the broader market context.

A question you might have is about timing – "when is the right time to invest?" Let's be clear: attempting to time the market perfectly is notoriously difficult, even for seasoned professionals. A more prudent strategy is to invest regularly, an approach known as dollar-cost averaging. It reduces the risk of investing a large amount in unfavorable conditions and smooths out the average purchase price over time.

Dividends are another pleasant feature of the stock market. Some companies distribute a portion of their profits to shareholders in the form of dividends. While not all stocks offer dividends, those that do provide a regular income stream, which can be reinvested or used as you see fit.

Being well-informed and mindful about the stock market lays the groundwork for making judicious investment choices. Remember, knowledge is power and power translates to success in the market. Whether you are looking to aggressively grow your wealth or seeking stable, longer-term investments, the stock market has a place for every woman on the spectrum of financial goals.

So, let's embrace the market not as a daunting behemoth, but as a powerful tool for financial advancement. Its ever-shifting landscape offers a path for those who learn to navigate its winds, enabling us to stake our claim in the world of investments and secure financial independence. As we endeavor into this realm, let's carry ourselves with confidence, armed with the wisdom to make choices that not only enrich our bank accounts but also our lives.

Building a Diversified Investment Portfolio Imagine a table set for a lavish meal, each dish offering a different flavor, texture, and nutrient. That's the essence of a diversified investment portfolio—it incorporates various types of investments to reduce risk and optimize returns, much like a balanced diet contributes to overall health. But don't let the jargon intimidate you; building a diversified portfolio can be as straightforward as hosting a potluck—everyone brings something different to the table, ensuring a range of tastes and a successful meal.

Diversification might sound elaborate, but it's just a fancy term for not putting all those hard-earned eggs into one basket. It's about spreading your investments across different asset classes, such as stocks, bonds, real estate, and perhaps more niche markets like commodities or even trendy ETFs. This way, if one sector takes a hit, your entire portfolio isn't left reeling. Think of it as financial self-defense; just as you would diversify your wardrobe for all seasons, diversify your investments for the unpredictable climate of the markets.

Why diversify? Let's cut to the chase: certain investments zig when others zag. Stocks and bonds typically move in opposite directions, so including both in your portfolio can help smooth out the rough patches. It's akin to having both a classic little black dress for timeless events and a trendier piece for fun occasions—different styles for different occasions.

Now, within those asset classes, further diversification is key. Consider stocks: you wouldn't invest solely in tech stocks, right? A well-rounded approach includes tapping into various industries—technology, healthcare, finance, consumer goods, and more. This approach ensures that a downfall in any one sector doesn't capsize your financial ship.

Bonds can be exciting too, I promise. They're not just a 'safety blanket' for risky stock moves. There are corporate bonds, government bonds, and municipal bonds, each with unique features that can serve

72

your portfolio well. Including a mix can provide steady income and a comforting buffer on volatile days.

International investments are the globetrotters of your portfolio, inviting you to explore opportunities beyond your home country's borders. By including these, you're tapping into growth in different economies, which can be especially valuable when the domestic market might be struggling. They can be the spices that elevate a dish from good to exquisite!

Let's not forget about real estate and commodities. Owning property or REITs can provide a tangible asset that often appreciates over time, while stashing some wealth in commodities like gold or oil could hedge against inflation. They're the sturdy boots and the silk scarf, adding practicality and a touch of flair.

The market is bursting with investment opportunities—mutual funds, index funds, exchange-traded funds (ETFs), and more. Mutual funds and ETFs can offer instant diversification, as they pool money from many investors to buy a broad portfolio of stocks, bonds, or other securities. Think of them as the investment equivalent of a fashion collection, where each piece contributes to the overall beauty of the line.

So, how do you start? Start small and start with what you know. You can always build up your portfolio as you gain confidence and knowledge. And it's okay to ask for help. A financial advisor can be an excellent guide, just like a personal stylist who helps you define your look.

Rebalancing is the final touch. Over time, certain investments might outgrow others, skewing your originally intended allocation. Periodically checking in on your portfolio to readjust it back to your desired balance is like decluttering your closet—keeping only what fits and serves you best.

Risks? Sure, they exist. But remember, by diversifying, you're lowering your investment risk overall. Think of it as a group of friends walking you home at night—it's safer together than going it alone.

Lastly, never lose sight of your goals. Your investment portfolio is a dynamic tool crafted to match your financial objectives, whether that's buying a house, starting a business, or sipping margaritas on a beach in retirement. Let it grow and adjust with you as your needs and the market change.

You've laid the groundwork for financial savvy in previous chapters, learning to save, budget, and understand debt. With those skills in hand, you're now ready to embark on the next crucial step toward financial independence: constructing a robust and diversified investment portfolio. Empower yourself with the confidence to mix and match your investments, and you might just find the journey to wealth as enjoyable as the destination itself.

- A flourishing financial future is not reserved for the few but open for everyone willing to embrace the diversity of the investment world. Whether you're putting your best foot forward in a well-kept pair of designer heels or comfortable, yet chic loafers, ensure your investment steps are as diverse and deliberate as your fashion choices. Here's to building a portfolio that complements your financial style as flawlessly as a tailored blazer on a Monday morning.

Chapter 10:
Protecting Your Assets -
The Ins and Outs of Insurance

Stepping smartly from the realm of growing your wealth *into* safeguarding it, we wade into the world of insurance with clarity and purpose. Think of insurance as that unshakeable friend, the one who's got your back when life throws its curveballs. You've worked hard for your assets; now let's talk about wrapping them in a security blanket so cozy, you'll sleep like a baby. Whether it's a fender bender or a medical misadventure, having the right coverage can be the difference between a minor hiccup and a financial freefall. We're diving into the types of insurance that matter most—from health to home, and beyond—because understanding the nuances can mean keeping your financial foundation strong. We'll navigate this together, unraveling the complexities, so you can craft a shield that's as resilient and dynamic as you are. Insurance isn't just another bill; it's an investment in your peace of mind, and darling, you're worth it.

Types of Insurance Coverage Now that you've laid the groundwork for a strong financial future with smart budgeting, saving, investing, and debt management techniques, let's delve into the array of insurance coverage options available to protect you and your assets. Insurance isn't just a safety net; it's a strategic move towards comprehensive financial planning. Let's explore, without delay, the diverse types of coverage you might consider including in your financial wardrobe.

Let's start with life's foundation: *health insurance*. This isn't just about visiting the doctor without fear of a hefty bill; it's about maintaining your well-being and, by extension, your financial health. Health insurance can cover everything from preventive care to major surgeries, and with options like High-Deductible Health Plans paired with Health Savings Accounts, you've got both protection and a savvy saving strategy at your disposal.

Another pillar of protection is *life insurance*. This type of coverage is about securing peace of mind for you and providing for your loved ones if the unexpected happens. With term life insurance providing focused coverage for a set period or whole life insurance offering a permanent solution plus a cash value component, it's an essential element of your long-term wealth-building strategy.

The importance of *disability insurance* cannot be understated. In the event that you are unable to work due to illness or injury, this insurance can be the bridge that maintains your lifestyle and financial obligations. With options like short-term and long-term disability, make sure you're prepared for whatever curveballs life might throw your way.

When you think about your home, it's not just four walls and a roof—it's a haven, a substantial investment, and a part of your financial portfolio. That's why *homeowners' insurance* is vital. It protects your abode against damage, theft, and sometimes even liability for accidents that occur on your property. And for those fabulous ladies of the renting world, don't overlook *renters' insurance* for protecting your personal belongings and providing liability coverage.

Now, let's talk about getting from point A to B. Your vehicle is more than just a mode of transportation; it's a part of your daily life's operational backbone. Protect it with *auto insurance*. Not only is this legally required in most places, but the right policy will cover costs associated with accidents, theft, and other vehicular misfortunes.

As we float into another consideration, consider the value of *flood insurance*. Standard homeowners' policies often do not cover flood damage, and with climate change increasing the frequency of extreme weather events, it's a wise addition to your financial umbrella.

For those who travel—whether it's for the glam getaways or the business trips—*travel insurance* is a must. This coverage can help reimburse you for non-refundable travel expenses, offer assistance during emergencies abroad, and even cover medical expenses if you fall ill while sipping that margarita on a sunny beach far from home.

Heading back to work, there's *professional liability insurance*, critical for those who run their own businesses or provide professional services. Protect yourself from claims of negligence or harm due to the services you provide, and keep your professional reputation gleaming.

Even when you're joyously planning for a wedding or hosting a charitable event, *event insurance* can save the day if things go awry. Sometimes events must be cancelled or liabilities occur; with event insurance, you won't be left holding the financial bag.

Moving up the ladder, let's consider your future with *long-term care insurance*. This coverage supports you in the event that you require assistance with daily living activities in your golden years. Don't underestimate the potential costs of care as you age—this insurance can be a linchpin in preserving your assets for you and your family.

And let's not forget about our furry or feathered family members! *Pet insurance* is becoming increasingly popular as veterinary costs rise. Protect your wallet from unexpected pet health emergencies, and make sure you can always provide the best care for your four-legged (or two-winged) companions.

For the savvy investors diversifying into rental properties, *landlord insurance* is the tool to ensure your investment properties are covered against damage, liability, and potential loss of rental income. It's custom-tailored armor for your real estate ventures.

A more niche—but no less important—type of insurance is *identity theft protection*. In our digital age, your personal information is valuable currency, and ensuring its safety is as important as locking your front door. Preventive measures and coverage after theft can both be vital in keeping your identity your own.

Now, as you approach or live out retirement, *annuities* can be a form of insurance worth discussing. They're like a DIY pension plan, turning your nest egg into a steady stream of income for the future. With fixed, variable, and indexed options, annuities can be tailored to your retirement vision.

The world of insurance can be as broad and varied as the wardrobes we cherish. With each type of insurance, you're not just paying for a service; you're investing in your peace of mind, safeguarding your future, and ensuring that whatever life throws at you, you'll remain unshakable. Just as you curate your wardrobe according to your style and needs, tailor your insurance portfolio to fit your unique life and goals. You have the power and the knowledge—use it to protect what matters most to you.

How Much Insurance Do You Really Need? So you're on this financial journey, navigating the different facets of building your net worth and making sure your assets are protected, but now you've hit the proverbial fork in the road: insurance. 'How much do I actually need?' is a common question, and the answer varies depending on who you are, what you own, and what your future plans look like. Let's break it down in a way that's as chic and clever as the very moves that are going to lead you to financial independence.

Firstly, there's the baseline of insurance that virtually everyone should consider: health insurance. We often underestimate the potential high costs of medical care, but having adequate coverage is vital. And let's be real, a medical emergency without insurance can be financially devastating. Think about your health, your family history, and your lifestyle to determine the amount of coverage that makes sense for you. Remember, skimping on health insurance can lead to huge out-of-pocket expenses that could wipe out your savings faster than a shopping spree at a designer boutique.

Next up, let's talk about life insurance. It's not the most glamorous subject to think about, but it's a crucial piece of the puzzle, especially if others depend on your income. If you're a parent, a partner, or someone who holds the financial fort in any way, life insurance is that safety net that can maintain the lifestyle of your loved ones, even if you're not there to do it yourself. How much you need often depends on how much debt you have (think mortgage, car loans, etc.), how your family's lifestyle costs, and any future needs (like college education for kids).

When it comes to property insurance, whether you own or rent, you'll want coverage that aligns with the value of your possessions and level of risk you're willing to take on. For homeowners, a policy that covers the replacement value of your home is key. Renters shouldn't overlook insurance either; your landlord's policy likely won't cover your personal belongings. This is where taking a proper inventory of what you own becomes essential. You might be surprised at the value of what you've accumulated over time!

Then there's auto insurance. It's not just about the law; it's about protection against significant potential expenses from an accident. Your driving habits and the value of your car will dictate the level of coverage that best suits you. And let's not forget about liability coverage – because if you're at fault in an accident, you could be on the hook for more than just bumper repairs.

Don't forget disability insurance. Your ability to earn a steady income can be seen as your most valuable asset. But what happens if you suddenly can't work due to an illness or injury? That's where disability insurance steps in, offering you a portion of your income until you can return to work. The amount you need can usually be calculated by looking at your monthly expenses and any employer coverage you might have.

But wait, there's more to consider – like liability insurance. If you're building your empire, whether it's a business or a solid reputation in your profession, you want to guard against potential lawsuits. This is where umbrella insurance can play a superhero role, offering extra coverage on top of your auto or homeowner's policies.

Here's a reminder that insurance is not about fearing the worst; it's about preparing for the unexpected with poise and pragmatism. A solid insurance plan allows you to walk confidently into your future, stilettos and all, knowing you've got a financial cushion to fall back on if needed.

Long-term care insurance is another piece of the puzzle that is often overlooked. As we live longer, the likelihood that we'll need some form of long-term care increases. Care costs can be exorbitant, so having insurance to help cover these expenses can protect your savings and investments from becoming medical bill payments.

When deciding on coverage levels across the board, consider your net worth and the assets you're protecting. If you have a higher net worth, you might need more coverage than the average policy offers – this is where an umbrella policy could come in handy, especially if you've got a significant amount of savings and investments.

The deductible amounts you choose can also sway the decision on how much insurance to get. Higher deductibles usually mean lower premiums, but they also mean more out-of-pocket costs when you file a claim. Strike a balance between a deductible you can manage if something happens and a premium that won't cramp your monthly budget. This level of fine-tuning ensures that the insurance is working for you, not against you.

Remember, there's no such thing as one-size-fits-all insurance. You've got unique dreams, assets, and circumstances. The right amount of insurance for you isn't necessarily the same as for your best friend or coworker. It involves a bit of introspection, perhaps a heart-to-heart with a financial planner, and certainly a review of your financial goals and current status.

One more thing before you venture into the world to tailor your perfect insurance wardrobe: always review your policies annually. Life changes – it's exciting and terrifying all at once. Maybe you've bought a new home, had a baby, or started a new business. These milestones may require adjustments to your insurance coverage to ensure you're still walking on the safe side of the sidewalk.

Now, let's circle back to that ever-pertinent question: how much insurance do you truly need? It's enough to provide a financial safety net but not so much that you're overpaying for protection you don't need. It's about balancing the premiums with the peace of mind.

Finally, as you sashay down this runway of life, let's make insurance your invisible cape. It may not be the most glittering accessory in your financial arsenal, but it will undoubtedly be one of the most critical. Your empowerment comes not just from the assets you accumulate, but also from the savvy steps you take to protect them. So, embrace that insurance policy like the protective shield it is, and let it be the unsung hero of your financial success story.

Chapter 11:
From Paychecks to Power -
Negotiation and Career Growth

As we shift focus from ensuring our assets are well-protected, let's dive into turning our paychecks into real power through astute negotiation and intentional career growth. Imagine entering a room where the stakes are high, your palms are sweaty, but your spirit is unyielding—you're there to negotiate your worth. It's about articulating your value with clarity and confidence, aiming for salary leaps instead of tiptoes. But we're not just talking about a one-time salary negotiation; this chapter is about embracing the growth mindset that'll have you climbing the career ladder with finesse. You'll learn not only to voice your worth but also to map out a career trajectory that aligns with your financial dreams and professional aspirations. Whether you're angling for that promotion, seeking out leadership roles, or navigating office dynamics, you'll find that career progression and financial empowerment go hand-in-hand. Let's channel that inner fortitude, because when it comes to your career, you're not just in it for the ride—you're steering the ship.

Negotiating Your Salary and Raises Transitioning from the landscape of investments to the personal strides we can make in our careers, let's hone in on a subject that can stimulate both personal and financial growth: negotiating your salary and raises. It's about chiseling your worth in the workforce and ensuring your paycheck reflects not just the work you do but also the value you contribute.

First, grasp the art of timing. A golden rule in successful negotiations is knowing when to initiate the conversation. Typically, this moment could be after completing a significant project superbly or during a performance review cycle. However, understand that companies often plan their budgets well in advance, so kickstarting the dialogue a few months prior can be strategically beneficial.

Preparation is your power suit in this scenario. Before entering this discussion, research is key. Equip yourself with knowledge about industry standards, salary ranges for your position, and what peers in similar roles are earning. Having these informative arrows in your quiver will show your employer that you're serious and justified in your request.

Now, let's conquer the confidence conundrum. Ladies, the jitters are normal, but remember, self-assurance is compelling. Expressing your contributions numerically can significantly support your case. So document your achievements, present figures that exhibit your accomplishments, and show how you've been instrumental in driving results.

Elevate your worth even further by expanding on not just what you've done, but what you can do. Share your vision for your role and your future contributions. Companies invest in potential, so paint a vivid picture of your professional trajectory and its alignment with the company's goals.

On to the negotiations themselves—don't just think about the base salary. An increase in compensation doesn't necessarily have to come only in the form of currency. Negotiate for benefits that are meaningful to you, whether that's flexible working hours, additional vacation days, a professional development budget, or perhaps a clearer pathway for progression.

When it comes to numbers, have a range rather than a single figure. By setting an acceptable spectrum, you leave room for discussion and prevent yourself from being anchored to a lower number than you deserve. However, make sure your range is realistic, yet aspirational—it's a delicate dance between asking for what you're worth and maintaining realistic expectations.

If the answer isn't the 'yes' you've been hoping for, don't be disheartened. Use this as an opportunity to ask "what's next?" Inquire about what you can achieve in order to be considered for a raise in the future. Constructive feedback paves the way for growth, and understanding where you can improve is invaluable for future negotiations.

Be ready to compromise but know your deal-breakers. It's essential to recognize the point at which an offer may no longer meet your needs or reflect your value. However, equally important is demonstrating flexibility and openness to finding a middle ground that benefits both you and your employer.

Remember, silence is a strategic tool. There's power in pausing after receiving an offer or counteroffer. Give yourself a moment to reflect and avoid the immediate urge to acquiesce or refute. This silent interlude can prompt your employer to divulge more information or a better offer.

Communication is the beating heart of negotiating. It's not just about what you say but how you say it. Maintain a positive tone, show enthusiasm for your role and the company, and stay level-headed, even if you start to feel anxious. The goal isn't just to secure a raise but to preserve and improve work relationships.

Post-negotiation, whether you walk away with a win or a promise for a future consideration, penning a thank-you note is a sophisticated touch. It expresses your appreciation for the time and effort your employer took to consider your request, and it solidifies your professionalism.

Keep the negotiation dialogue open by setting a date for a follow-up conversation. This not only shows initiative but also illustrates your commitment to growth and continuous improvement. Frame this as a checkpoint to review your performance and revisit the potential for compensation enhancement.

Lastly, if you reach an impasse and the compensation simply isn't on par with your worth - and researching, reflecting, and negotiating have demonstrated this clearly - it may be time to explore new horizons. Your financial growth can sometimes be accelerated in a new environment that recognizes and values your contributions fully.

Bringing all these strands together, negotiating your salary and raises becomes less daunting and more of a strategic engagement. It's an avenue to assert your value, express your professional aspirations, and potentially enhance your financial well-being. Invest time in mastering this skill, and the dividends it pays will be worth more than just a bump in your paycheck; it's about empowering your position and establishing your reputation as a professional invaluable enough to invest in.

Climbing the Corporate Ladder is an exhilarating challenge filled with opportunities and obstacles. As savvy women on the move, we've already learned the foundations of personal finance. Now, let's shift the focus to our careers and the concrete steps we can take to ascend the ranks, increase our earning potential, and expand our influence within the corporate world.

Before we delve into strategies for career advancement, let's begin by recognizing that, as women, we may face unique systemic hurdles. However, it's crucial to remember that we're not just navigating the

Scarlett Brooksgment>

corporate ladder; we're transforming it. Each rung we climb is a combination of our skill, creativity, and resilience.

First and foremost, it's about positioning oneself strategically. Identify your company's growth areas and align your skills with these segments. Being at the right place at the right time means being visible to those who can propel your career forward. Volunteer for new projects, especially those with high visibility, and always bring your A-game.

Mentorship is a secret weapon. A mentor can provide invaluable advice, introduce you to key players, and help navigate the often unwritten rules of corporate advancement. Seek out mentors within and outside your organization. Remember, mentorship is a two-way street – be prepared to bring something to the table.

Continuous learning is non-negotiable. Whether it's formal education, professional certifications, or self-directed learning, ensure you're up to date with the latest industry trends and skills. Investing in yourself is a message to the world that you're serious about your growth.

Constructive networking should not be underestimated. Attend industry events, join professional associations, and use every interaction to build your personal brand. Networking isn't just about taking; it's about creating genuine connections and finding ways to give back as well.

Say yes to leadership opportunities, even when they're outside your comfort zone. Understand that leadership isn't a title; it's a behavior. Each time you lead a team, a project, or a meeting, you demonstrate your potential to handle bigger responsibilities.

Always document your achievements. Maintain an updated career portfolio with a record of your projects, results, and acknowledgments.

86

This portfolio becomes indispensable during evaluations or when discussing promotions.

It's essential to assertively communicate your career aspirations to your superiors. Be clear about your goals and seek regular feedback. Strategic self-promotion helps ensure that decision-makers are aware of your contributions and ambitions.

Building a sponsor within your company can catapult your career to new heights. A sponsor is someone with power who will advocate for you when it comes to promotions or choice assignments. Unlike a mentor, a sponsor will actively push for your advancement.

Work-life balance is a key factor in long-term career success. Prioritizing your health and personal time isn't a sign of weakness; it's an integral part of sustaining your performance and preventing burnout.

Remember not to let setbacks derail you. When faced with failures or disappointments, see them as learning experiences. Failure is often the prelude to greater success and resilience is your companion every step of the way up the corporate ladder.

Finally, champion other women. When you grow your influence, use it to support and elevate others. This creates a ripple effect of empowerment and transforms your work environment into one where diversity is not just encouraged but celebrated.

In conclusion, let your ascent be guided by the values of excellence, integrity, and generosity. Climb not just for the title or the paycheck, but for the fulfillment of your potential, and to pave the way for the brilliant women who will follow.

As we move on to the next chapter, keep the lessons from this journey at the forefront. Whether you're eyeing the C-suite or carving out a niche of expertise, remember that your career growth contributes significantly to your overall financial empowerment.

Chapter 12:
Entrepreneurial Elegance -
Starting Your Own Business

You've got a fiery spirit and a vision that just won't quit—and now's the time to transform that energy into your very own enterprise. Stepping into the entrepreneurial arena might just be the smartest move for your financial future and personal fulfillment. Imagine being the master of your destiny, breaking free from the constraints of the 9-to-5, and seeing your name emblazoned on a business that reflects your passion and perseverance. Starting your business is about harnessing your unique talents and carving out a niche that no one else can fill quite like you can. It's about fine-tuning a dream into a business plan that's as chic as it is savvy, lining up resources that will back you up when you need it most, and polishing your brand until it shines bright in the marketplace. Tailor your path with finesse; create a symphony of services or products that the world just can't wait to experience. This chapter is all about lifting the veil on entrepreneurship and guiding you through the exquisite journey of starting your own business, with the grace and confidence of a seasoned CEO. With a touch of creativity, a dash of courage, and a clear financial blueprint, you're ready to leap into the thrilling world of entrepreneurship.

The Basics of Entrepreneurship If you're poised to take charge of your financial destiny, understanding the essence of entrepreneurship might just be your golden ticket. Let's unravel the threads of starting your own business—one of the boldest financial and personal moves you can make. Encapsulated within entrepreneurship are passion, vision, and the grit to transform ideas into reality. To get you on the right track, let's begin with some cornerstones for initiating this exhilarating journey.

Firstly, recognize that entrepreneurship is more than just a financial pursuit; it's a mindset. It's the fortitude to stand at the helm of your ship, weathering storms and navigating through uncharted waters. Embracing this mentality means being willing to take risks and pivot when necessary—qualities that are quintessential for any successful entrepreneur.

Delineating the idea is where it all starts. This is often birthed from a combination of noticing a need and the burning desire to address it. Your first step is to ask yourself what problem you're determined to solve and whether your solution fills a gap in the market. If you're fueled by a unique concept that serves a specific niche or broadens an existing market, you're already on the path.

Once the idea crystalizes, it's time to sculpt it into a viable business model. This is where strategy comes into play. How will your enterprise create value? How will it earn revenue? These are the pillars of your business plan, a document that frames the blueprint of your venture and something you can present to potential investors or partners.

Don't overlook the importance of understanding your target audience. Know who your customers are, what they need, and where to find them. This vital reconnaissance informs your marketing strategy, helping to ensure that your message aligns with the people most likely to buy into your vision.

Marketing may seem daunting, but in this digital age, it's also more accessible than ever. Whether it's through social media, a well-designed website, or grassroots networking, marketing is the megaphone that transforms your whispers into roars and brings your brand to life.

Funding, the lifeblood of any new venture, is something you'll need to secure early. Whether it's through savings, loans, investors, or crowdfunding, securing capital is vital. It's also a test of your conviction, as you'll have to convince others that your idea is worth their financial backing.

Operational logistics can't be understated either. You'll need to consider the legal structure of your business, whether that be sole proprietorship, partnership, limited liability company (LLC), or corporation. Each comes with its own set of implications for liability, taxes, and control. Take time to find what fits your business goals and personal liability comfort level.

Speaking of taxes, they can be a labyrinth for the uninitiated. Nevertheless, it's crucial to get your head around the basics, like the different types of taxes you'll be responsible for and what deductions you can claim. A good accountant can be worth their weight in gold here.

As a business owner, you're also the chief officer of human resources—particularly in the early days when you're possibly the CEO and the janitor. Hiring the right people who share your vision and work ethic can drive your business forward. Likewise, knowing when and how to delegate is a crucial leadership skill that allows you to focus on growth-oriented activities.

Grit and resilience are two traits you'll hear about often in entrepreneurial circles. Know that failure is not the opposite of success in this realm—it's a part of it. Each setback is an opportunity to learn and refine your strategies. Persevere, pivoting where necessary, and your venture will be all the stronger for it.

Never underestimate the value of a solid network. Connections can lead to advice, support, and even new business. Build relationships with mentors, join relevant groups, and attend industry events. Your network can be the support system that helps sustain you through tough times and a source for opportunities that propel you during periods of growth.

Entrepreneurship isn't for the faint of heart, but then again, neither is striving for financial independence. It's a path that can lead to unparalleled personal growth and financial liberation. By making financial literacy your bedrock, integrating savvy planning, and harnessing your unique talents, your business can flourish.

In this eloquent dance of entrepreneurship, balance is key. There will be times when your business demands long hours and times when your well-being requires stepping back. As you navigate this journey, remember that your greatest asset is you—with your health, determination, and continuous learning, your entrepreneurial story unfolds.

To sum up, the foundation of entrepreneurship is equal parts exciting and daunting. It rests on your shoulders to kindle the spark of your idea into a flame. It demands relentless passion, meticulous planning, and a wealth of courage. But for those who are up for the challenge, the rewards can be extraordinary—not just in financial terms, but in the autonomy and fulfillment that come from building something truly your own.

Funding Your Business Venture Kicking off a business venture requires more than just a brilliant idea and a dose of enthusiasm; it demands financial fuel to turn dreams into tangible results. Let's talk dollars and sense—specifically, how you can secure the funds necessary to launch and sustain your venture.

The most straightforward path you might envision is using your savings. Self-funding or bootstrapping has the perk of autonomy—no debts, no external stakeholders breathing down your neck. But before you drain your savings account, consider this: keeping a financial buffer for personal emergencies is crucial. Dipping into personal funds is an option, yet, striking a balance to maintain financial safety is essential.

Then, there are friends and family. The people who believe in you might also bank on your success. Raising funds from your inner circle sounds comfortable, but it comes with its own caveats. Ensure you approach it with a clear agreement to keep relationships intact—preferably with the same rigor as you would with an outside investor.

What about loans? Traditional bank loans are a common source for funding, but you'll need to have a solid business plan and credit history. Ladies, the paperwork and process might seem daunting, but it's feasible with the right preparation. And there are various loan programs designed to assist women entrepreneurs.

Another avenue is finding an angel investor, those visionary individuals who offer capital for startups in exchange for ownership equity or convertible debt. Network at industry events, join entrepreneurial communities, or use online platforms to connect with potential angels. It's your chance to find a financial guardian for your business.

Speaking of networking, venture capital could also be a means to your end. VCs typically want to invest in high-growth companies with a clear exit strategy, so it's crucial to have a solid pitch and understand the strings attached regarding control and decision-making.

Crowdfunding has democratized business funding in many ways. Platforms like Kickstarter or Indiegogo can offer a unique way to raise money while validating your business idea. It's about creating a compelling story about your brand that resonates with potential backers. Get creative and engage the crowd!

If you're pondering the possibility of grants, well, there's good news! There are numerous grants available specifically for women entrepreneurs. These can be golden opportunities as they don't require repayment. Research diligently, apply widely, and remember, every bit counts.

Let's not forget about the potential within incubators and accelerators. These programs can provide capital, mentoring, and valuable business resources. They might take some equity, but the trade-off is often knowledge, networking, and a stronger growth trajectory.

And there's government support too. The Small Business Administration offers various loan programs that might suit your venture. Their mission is to empower entrepreneurs, and they might be your gateway to the financial backing you need.

Influencers and brand partnerships can also play unexpected roles in your funding strategy. A strong brand collaboration or an endorsement from an influencer can jumpstart your business's visibility, leading to more sales and investment interest.

Suppose you're in the technology or innovation field. In that case, research and development grants, or even competitions, can be a robust financing source. They may require an intense application process, but the rewards can be substantial and often not limited to just finance alone.

For the side hustler ready to transition to full-time entrepreneurship, remember that your side gigs can be a great source of capital. It's having your cake and eating it too—earning while building your business funds and testing the entrepreneurial waters.

Lastly, never underestimate the power of bartering and strategic partnerships. Lower initial costs by exchanging services, or enter into alliances that can help defer costs in exchange for long-term relationships or equity.

Regardless of your chosen path, remember to maintain a clear vision and remain tenacious. Funding your business can feel overwhelming, but with the proper approach, you can navigate this exciting stage. You have the potential to sculpt a financial plan that works not just for your business, but also aligns with your personal values and financial future. Here's to your success—as you invest in your business, you're investing in yourself, too.

Chapter 13:
Tax Tactics - Understanding Taxes and Deductions

Moving from the entrepreneurial spirit to the nitty-gritty of tax season, it's essential to peel back the layers of what can often feel like a daunting topic: taxes and deductions. Now, let's take this journey one step further by diving into the empowering world of tax knowledge. You've got this! Understanding the structure of taxes isn't just about paying your dues; it's about mastering the art of keeping your hard-earned money where it belongs—in your wallet. As you explore this chapter, you'll uncover the secrets behind effective tax strategies, gain insights into how deductions can work in your favor, and learn how to navigate the maze of tax codes with poise and confidence. Remember, when it comes to taxes, you're not at the mercy of a confusing system; you're in command, making informed decisions that align with your financial goals. It's not just about getting through tax season; it's about coming out on top, with more resources to invest in your future.

Navigating Tax Season with Confidence Let's dive into a topic that can make many of us feel like we're wading through murky waters: tax season. It's that period when the thought of W-2s, deductions, and the IRS looming can cause genuine anxiety. But guess what? It doesn't have to be a stress marathon. You're going to navigate tax season with poise and assurance because, honestly, you're fully capable of tackling this head-on.

Tax season is much like a puzzle, and you hold all the pieces. Start by gathering every necessary document: your income statements, possibly 1099s if you've done any freelance work, and receipts for deductible expenses. Think of it as a financial year in review—a chance to see the complete picture of your earnings and where you've invested your hard-earned cash.

Let's talk about deadlines. Usually, taxes are due in mid-April, but keep a close eye on the calendar because the exact date can shift if it falls on a weekend or holiday. Missing the deadline can lead to unnecessary penalties, and we're all about dodging those extra costs with a little foresight.

Coming to terms with terminology can be a bit like learning a new language. However, terms like 'adjusted gross income,' 'tax credits,' and 'deductions' are now part of your financial vocabulary. Understanding what these terms mean is critical because they directly impact how much tax you'll pay—or how much of a refund you might receive, which is always a silver lining.

It's empowering to realize that you can reduce your taxable income legally. This can be done by maximizing your contributions to retirement accounts such as your 401(k) or an IRA. Doing this not only sets you up for future richness, but it can provide immediate tax benefits.

Now, about those nebulous tax deductions and credits—this is where attention to detail pays off. There are deductions for educational expenses, charitable contributions, and even for the home office you've set up. Credits can be even more tantalizing because they reduce your tax bill dollar-for-dollar. Having knowledge of these benefits can transform your tax situation from owing to getting a nice refund.

If you're feeling overwhelmed with the complexities of the tax code, remember that there's no shame in seeking guidance—from trusted tax professionals or reliable software that walks you through every step. Feel the power in enlisting help to ensure you're executing everything correctly. You wouldn't go to a ball without the right dress; why tackle taxes without the right tools?

Filing electronically is like swapping snail mail for a sleek jet. It's faster, more secure, and typically gets you your refund quicker if you're expecting one. Direct deposit is the cherry on top, placing your refund directly into your bank account. Hassle-free and quick—that's what we're aiming for.

Some tax situations are more complex than others, especially if you're an entrepreneur or have multiple streams of income. Dive into understanding the tax implications of your business structure, or speak with a professional who can guide you to tax-savvy decisions throughout the year—not just in April.

For the savvy investor, remember that capital gains tax and dividends play a part in your overall fiscal picture. Long-term and short-term gains are taxed differently, and depending on what investments you have, you might need to pay particular attention to these details. Keep meticulous records, and yes, this can underscore the importance of your investment choices in terms of tax implications.

Audits are an aspect of tax season that can cause unnecessary worry. Maintain accurate records throughout the year and be truthful on your returns. With integrity as your shield, there's no reason to fear an audit. Consider it a verification process that you're prepared to pass with flying colors because you've kept things in immaculate order.

If you do find yourself owing taxes and it's an amount that isn't easy to conjure up, don't panic. The IRS offers payment plans. It's essential not to ignore the situation because, as with all things financial, pretending a problem doesn't exist won't make it vanish. Proactively managing what you owe demonstrates responsibility and can save you from escalated stress in the long run.

Now, perhaps you're on the other side of the coin—the lucky recipient of a tax refund. While it might be tempting to view this as free money ripe for splurging, consider allocating your refund toward your financial goals. Whether it's bolstering your emergency fund, paying down debt, or investing for the future, using this "bonus" strategically can amplify your financial journey.

Refining your understanding of tax laws, staying organized, and crafting a plan for either paying what you owe or investing your refund puts you in control. Our goal isn't just to survive tax season but to approach it with finesse. Let the thought of tackling taxes energize rather than intimidate you. With every form you fill out and every deduction you claim, you're honing your financial acumen.

The final piece of advice is to keep your pulse on any changes to tax laws. By staying informed, you ensure that you're not missing out on new opportunities to minimize your tax liability or to take advantage of new tax credits and deductions. Legislation can change from year to year, and being in the know is part of maintaining your financial edge.

By approaching tax season with a strategy, a calm mind, and a bit of planning, you'll cross the finish line with confidence. You've got more power over your taxes than you might think. Remember, tax season isn't just about meeting legal obligations—it's an integral part of your overall financial well-being, and you're managing it like the financial maven you are.

Maximizing Deductions and Credits can feel like navigating a labyrinth with a broken compass. But with some savvy insights and a dash of moxie, you'll find this journey can lead to some serious savings at tax time. We're here to link arms and walk you through this maze, ensuring you come out on the other side feeling empowered, not exasperated.

First off, think of deductions as the universe's little way of giving you a discount on your taxable income. Yes, they're a gift – so let's unwrap them properly. Itemized deductions are the fancy shoes of the tax world; they require a bit more work to pull off, but when you do, they can truly elevate your financial outfit. We're talking about things like mortgage interest, charitable donations, and medical expenses that exceed a certain portion of your income. Take stock of your expenditures throughout the year and keep those receipts; they're the golden tickets to your deduction fiesta.

Now, credits – these aren't just discounts. They're dollar-for-dollar reductions in your tax bill, and who doesn't love a good deal? Some credits are refundable, meaning even if you owe zero in taxes, the government will pay you the difference. From the Earned Income Tax Credit to the Child and Dependent Care Credit, these are the VIP passes of tax season. Understanding what's available to you is crucial in capitalizing on these benefits.

Education can unlock many doors, and tax credits are no exception. If you're paying for college expenses, the American Opportunity Credit and the Lifetime Learning Credit can be a goldmine. They target different phases of education, so understanding which one fits your journey can really pay off – literally! And let's not forget about state-specific credits too. Some states offer unique benefits for everything from green home improvements to education savings accounts, so it pays to know your local tax landscape.

Ever heard of above-the-line deductions? These are your front-of-the-line passes, subtracted from your income before you even get to those itemized or standard decisions. Contributions to traditional IRAs, student loan interest, and educator expenses are all waiting for you there. Embrace these goodies; they'll slim down your taxable income before you even get to the main tax meal.

Business owners, listen up! Every expense that goes into running your empire could potentially be deductible. From start-up costs to a portion of your internet bill, make sure every dime you're entitled to is accounted for. As for you side hustlers, this applies to you too! A dash of organization through the year will save you from a headache when tax season rolls around.

Did you know there are credits specifically to reward you for being eco-friendly? That's right – installing solar panels or driving an electric vehicle can let you cash in on tax benefits. Mother Earth and your wallet will thank you for taking advantage of these green incentives. It's like strutting down the environmental runway while securing some financial flair with each step.

Let's chat retirement for a quick second – contributing to retirement accounts like your 401(k) or IRA doesn't just prepare you for a beachy retirement. It can also reduce your taxable income now! That's a win-win in anyone's book. Just remember there are limits to these contributions, so keep an eye on them as part of your tax strategizing.

Childcare can be as expensive as the latest designer bag. Thankfully, the government offers some help here too. The Child Tax Credit can alleviate a chunk of what it costs to raise those little ones. And don't overlook the potential for additional state credits related to your children – these can vary, so do your homework and see what your state offers.

Health Savings Accounts (HSAs) and Flexible Spending Accounts (FSAs) are not just great for your health; they're kind to your taxes, too. Contributions to these accounts are tax-deductible, and withdrawals for qualified medical expenses are tax-free. Stash some cash and pump up your health without getting taxed on it? Yes, please!

Many people miss out on work-related deductions. If you're spending money on uniforms, union dues, or job-related education that your employer isn't reimbursing you for, these might be deductible. Think of these as investing in your career's wardrobe – essential and potentially tax-friendly.

The real trick in maximizing deductions and credits isn't just about knowing what they are – it's about strategizing throughout the year. By planning ahead, you can maximize charitable contributions or delay income to a year where it'll be taxed at a lower rate – all fair game in the tax world. It's the equivalent of timing your fashion purchases for when the sales hit – smart and totally satisfying.

What about those changes rumbling through life? Getting married, having a baby, or buying a home might not just be personal milestones but also substantial tax landmarks. Shifts in life mean shifts in taxes; so keep abreast of how each life event can alter your tax situation.

Lastly, staying informed and seeking guidance can be like hiring a top-notch stylist for your financial wardrobe. A tax professional can help you identify deductions and credits you didn't even know you had access to, just like a great stylist finds those hidden gems in your closet. It's all about getting the most out of your assets.

Remember, the goal is to never leave money on the table. Taxes can take a chunk out of our finances, but with a little acumen and a lot of awareness, you can keep more of your hard-earned money where it belongs – in your purse. So as you gracefully tiptoe through tax laws and provisions, you'll be less worried about the tax bite and more focused on how fabulous financial empowerment feels!

Chapter 14:
Love and Money - Managing
Finances in Relationships

When love intertwines with finances, the results can be as complicated as a triple-knotted statement necklace. Just as we've built a foundation of financial self-empowerment throughout our journey, in this chapter we turn the lens towards tandem fiscal fitness within relationships. Let's talk brass tacks: being on the same page with your significant other about money matters isn't just nice—it's non-negotiable for long-term harmony. From the butterflies of a new relationship to the steadfast unions that can weather any storm, every stage brings its own set of financial syncopation to master. We're not just hinting at who picks up the dinner tab on date night, but digging into the hearty discussions that mold our shared financial futures. Whether you're navigating the early days of joint budget blues or sailing in the more mature waters of retirement planning together, crafting a game plan that reflects both your dreams and your practicalities is key. And let's shatter the taboo: yes, talking prenups, co-managing debts and investments, and aligning on spending habits may seem about as romantic as cold coffee, but they're essential ingredients in the recipe for relationship success. After all, joining forces in love should also mean building an unshakable financial team—that's the kind of power couple we're here to become.

Financial Conversations with Your Partner As we gracefully navigate the complexities of our financial journeys, nothing quite compares to the dance of aligning our money moves with those of a significant other. Entering into uncharted territory of joint finances can feel daunting, but it needn't be a tango of turmoil if we approach it with the right mindset and tools. And it starts with the cornerstone of any great relationship: communication.

Imagine sipping your favorite coffee blend across from your partner, both ready to unfold the figures and dreams each has scribbled on note pads or locked away in thoughts. These conversations shouldn't be reserved for dire straits; they're essential in times of calm and should bubble up naturally, early, and often in the relationship. They set the stage for trust, understanding, and synchronicity in your shared financial future.

Laying out your financial landscape can be revealing and incredibly intimate. It encompasses your earnings, savings, investments, debts, and not to overlook, your financial aspirations and fears. Be candid about your financial history and current standing. Sharing openly helps your partner understand your perspective and provides a solid ground for planning ahead together.

Speaking of planning, goals must make their way into these chats. Do you pine for a cozy cottage by the lake, or are you gunning for a penthouse with cityscape views? Are children in the picture? Will there be goldendoodles or tabby cats? Triumphs in these discussions lie not only in dreaming up a future but also laying clear paths to reach them. This is where you both can leverage your individual strengths to propel your financial journey.

The honey on the spoon is the budget talk. Budgets aren't shackles; think of them as your savvy financial GPS systems. When you're armed with a shared budget, you can guide your spending and saving with confidence and clarity. It matters not if you're thrift store aficionados or if fine dining is your splurge of choice—it's about ensuring your outlays align with your combined goals.

Debt—it's the pesky third wheel no one invited but tends to tag along anyway. Addressing this upfront can alleviate pressure and prevent grievances from festering. Consolidate, eradicate, celebrate—this could be the mantra for dealing with debt jointly. And remember, it's "our" debt now, not just "yours" or "mine."

When dreams are on the line, protection is paramount. Insurance might seem like a snooze fest, but it's actually your financial safety net. Discuss the types and levels of coverage that'll cradle your collective aspirations. This is love in its most pragmatic form—caring about each other's peace of mind.

Retirement may seem like a distant serenade, but it's one tune you'll want to learn the lyrics to together ASAP. What do you both envision for your golden years? Yachts, philanthropy, or tranquil cottage living? Starting early gives you the magic of compounding and more time to tweak the plan, making it track with your life's rhythm.

One marked distinction that will ground these conversations is understanding that it's more than a sharing of facts and figures; it's also sharing responsibility, power, and respect for each other's influence in financial decisions. This encompasses everything from the day-to-day transactions to the bigger bets like property investments and business ventures.

Expect hiccups; no duet is perfect from the get-go. Stay adaptable and patient. When one fumbles, the other is there to pick up the beat. The aim isn't to mimic each other's financial habits perfectly but to sync in a way that harmonizes your individual strengths and compensates for weaknesses.

And let's be clear—equality does not mean sameness. If one earns more, talk honestly about how that impacts your joint contributions towards shared goals. What matters is that you're both pulling in the same direction, whether through equal amounts or equal percentages of your income. Equality in a relationship is about equitable participation, respect, and decision-making.

Tricky subjects will surface, from prenups to inheritances. Embrace these talks; they're not foreboding omens but prudent steps. A prenup, for instance, might feel unromantic, but it's simply a protective clause for you both, especially if one enters the union with substantially more assets or debt. Plan for the best, prepare for the unexpected—it's wisdom at its financial best.

Financial fidelity is a phrase to live by. Just as you'd expect emotional faithfulness, financial faithfulness is key. This means no hidden accounts, no secret stashes (unless they're part of a delightful surprise), and no lies about spending or debt. It's the bedrock of trust in your financial relationship.

When children come into the picture or significant life changes occur, loop back to the drawing board. Refresh your financial plan, ensuring it's a snug fit for the new phase of life. A baby changes more than sleep cycles—it transforms financial priorities and strategies as well.

Lastly, remember that money is a tool to build a life you both cherish, not a scorecard of who contributes more. Strive for a relationship where assets grow not just in your bank accounts but in the trust, support, and shared visions between you and your partner. Open-hearted, open-minded conversations about money are where true financial intimacy blooms and where you both can flourish, empowered and in unison.

Now, as we leave the topic of partnership in finance, let's transition smoothly to the details surrounding the more technical aspects, like prenups, joint accounts, and the nuts and bolts of financial planning for couples. But remember, the foundation of it all lies within the quality and candor of your financial conversations.

Prenups, Joint Accounts, and Financial Planning
Transitioning from the heady winds of career ascendancy and entrepreneurial prowess, let's address a field that's a mix of romance and realism: the world of love meets money. Merging finances with your significant other is like a dance – it requires grace, communication, and a solid understanding of each party's movements. Before you set off on this tango, let's consider the value of a prenuptial agreement (prenup), the dynamics of joint accounts, and the essence of collaborative financial planning.

First, prenups. Far from signaling mistrust, think of them as a transformative tool for empowerment. Prenups offer clarity and protection, laying out terms that can help avoid messy disputes should the love story encounter an unexpected plot twist. It's a practical step, acknowledging that while you're planning a life together, you're also safeguarding your individual financial journeys. Engage in candid dialogues about assets, debts, and financial expectations. It's not semantics; it's about securing harmony as well as assets.

Onto joint accounts. They're about sharing and transparency, vital ingredients in any strong partnership. Yet, remember the age-old adage – don't put all your eggs in one basket. It's wise to maintain personal accounts alongside a joint one, assuring a safety net and a space for independent financial growth. Discuss expenditure rules, savings contributions, and how you'll navigate the murky waters of large purchases. This conversation can strengthen the trust and teamwork in your relationship.

Financial planning as a couple is not just about dreaming together; it's about activating those dreams. Set joint goals, be they purchasing a family home or planning dream vacations. Mark milestones and celebrate the small victories. Remember, just as you may compromise on dinner choices, financial planning will also involve give-and-take. Blend your financial personalities rather than letting them clash. You might be surprised how compatible a saver and a spender can be when they align their objectives.

Alas, some elements are better kept separate. Credit is one. Always maintain your own credit identity. A strong personal credit score will ensure you always have access to financial opportunities, regardless of your relational status. Joint debt, on the other hand, can be a strategic move for big joint ventures like homeownership, but tread carefully. Each step into shared debt should be as calculated as your solo investments.

Contemplate the notion of a financial planner. They're not just for the supremely wealthy. A professional can help manage those amalgamated funds and provide objective advice. As partners, you bring your unique attitudes towards money to the table, and a third-party expert can help mediate and mold a cohesive financial strategy.

If family planning is in your stars, let's address the elephant in the room – children are delightful yet costly little beings. A joint financial strategy should account for child-related expenses, from diapers to diplomas. Consider establishing education funds early on – you'll thank yourselves later. It's also an opportune moment to reflect on life insurance, to ensure that unforeseen circumstances won't undermine the financial well-being of the family.

While discussing children, and even if they're not yet in the picture, estate planning is crucial. Wills, trusts, and beneficiaries should be on your radar early in your union. It's not just about end-of-life scenarios; it's also about creating peace of mind, knowing that your collaborated wealth is distributed according to your shared desires.

Moreover, while on your philanthropic forays, remember charity begins at home. Set aside funds for joint charity, aligning your giving with shared values, and reinforcing the collective aspect of your financial union. This is as much about financial planning as it is about fostering a sense of unity and purpose within your relationship.

Let's not overlook the uncomfortable scenarios. In case of marital discord, it's crucial to know where you stand financially. Have open access to all financial documents and understand your joint financial landscape. Ignorance may be bliss, but in the realm of finances, knowledge is power – you want to be holding your own map in this journey.

There's a lyrical beauty to navigating these financial waters together. While it involves numerous logistical considerations, remember you're crafting a shared symphony, not just a list of transactions. It's an ongoing process, adjusting as life unfolds. Be patient with each other, and keep the communication channels as open as your hearts.

And so, in the realm of finances and romance, it's clear that love isn't blind – it's visionary. It peers into the future and builds a framework for prosperity grounded in mutual respect and individual autonomy. As you embark on this chapter of your financial journey, hold hands, but also respect that each has their own purse. Honor the individual dreams that contribute to a shared vision – it's the essence of true partnership.

Maintain a joyful anticipation for the future and reverence for the present. Embrace the dance of finances and romance, knowing that the steps you take are as much about individual growth as they are about moving in unison. By addressing prenups, joint accounts, and financial planning, you're not just setting financial goals, you're crafting a story of unity, security, and shared success.

Remember, combining your lives doesn't mean losing your financial identities. It's about creating a rich tapestry, interwoven with love, strategic financial choices, and a commitment to not just survive but thrive together. Forge ahead with confidence, ladies. Your joined financial journey is a canvas awaiting your mutual masterpiece.

Chapter 15:
Wealthy and Wise - Building
Generational Wealth

Transitioning from the pragmatic considerations of managing day-to-day finances and relationship dynamics, we now embark on a pivotal quest: the creation of generational wealth. This isn't just about padding your bank account; it's a crusade to lay the foundation for your family's financial future. Why just live for the moment when you can etch your legacy into the annals of time? The essence of wisdom comes from not only cultivating your own garden of wealth but nurturing the soil for the seeds of the next generation to flourish. Now, let's get down to brass tacks: it's about growing your assets to a point where they're not just surviving, but thriving through the decades. Think bigger picture; we're not only securing comfort for our retirement but for the kind of legacy that empowers our children and their children after them. And this isn't some lofty ideal out of reach for the average Jane - everyone's got the potential to contribute to a legacy, be it large or small. This chapter will serve as your roadmap, steering you towards avenues that foster wealth over the long haul, enabling you to pass on not just your values but a financial cushion that could softly land generations to come.

Estate Planning and Inheritance Strategies Now that we've delved into the power of building wealth, let's shift our focus to protecting it. Ensuring our hard-earned assets benefit loved ones requires thoughtful estate planning and savvy inheritance strategies. I want you to think of estate planning not as a grim task, but as a crucial step in affirming your legacy and safeguarding your financial wishes.

First up, a will is where it all begins. If you haven't already drafted one, make it your priority. A will clearly outlines who inherits your assets, from your favorite pearl necklace to your property assets. It's like giving your loved ones a roadmap to your wishes, easing their minds during a difficult time.

Consider a trust as a smart companion to your will. Certain trusts can shield your estate from the public eye and potential estate taxes, ensuring more of your wealth goes directly to those you care about most. It's not just for the ultra-wealthy; a trust can be a powerful tool for many, offering control over when and how your assets are distributed.

Life insurance is another cornerstone of estate planning. It provides a tax-free lump sum to your beneficiaries upon your passing, which can be essential for covering living expenses, tuition, or maintaining a business. Make sure your coverage matches your current lifestyle and responsibilities—it's about keeping promises to those who depend on you.

Designating beneficiaries is a must-do. Whether it's your retirement accounts, life insurance policies, or investment accounts, ensure that these are up-to-date. You wouldn't want your ex-partner accidentally receiving your 401(k) because of an oversight, would you?

And speaking of retirement accounts, certain types like Roth IRAs can be especially beneficial for inheritance purposes. The accounts grow tax-free, and distributions can also be tax-free, making them a sweet deal for anyone inheriting them. Make sure you understand the rules though, as they can change and may affect your estate planning strategy.

Now, let's talk about taxes. Estate or inheritance taxes can be significant, but with careful planning, their impact can be minimized. Simple steps, such as gifting portions of your wealth while you're still alive, up to the tax-free limit, can make a big impact. This not only reduces your taxable estate but also brings joy in seeing your loved ones benefit from your generosity now.

And remember, communication is key. Your estate plan is more than a set of documents; it's a conversation. Involve your loved ones in discussions about your intentions. A family meeting can clear up questions and align expectations, reducing the chance of conflict after you're gone. It's about leaving a legacy of harmony, not just wealth.

For the business owners among you, succession planning is crucial. You've put blood, sweat, and tears into your business; now ensure it thrives beyond you. Whether you're passing it down or selling it, have a plan that supports your employees, your legacy, and your family's needs.

Don't forget about digital assets. We live in a digital age, with online accounts and social media presence. Make provisions for who manages them and how. These are personal reflections of you and are part of your estate just as much as a physical asset.

Healthcare directives are also an aspect of estate planning. Assign someone who understands your wishes for medical care if you can't express them. It's tough but necessary to discuss, and it can save your family additional stress in dire situations.

Consider working with an estate planning attorney. It might seem like an extra cost now, but it's an investment in peace of mind. They'll help you navigate complex laws, providing a customized plan that fits the nuances of your life. Remember, estate planning isn't one-size-fits-all, and expert guidance can be invaluable.

Philanthropy can also play a role in your estate plan. If there's a cause dear to your heart, you can establish a legacy that echoes your values through charitable trusts or donations. It's a way to keep your spirit alive, impacting the world positively, even when you're no longer here.

Lastly, keep your estate plan updated. Life changes like marriage, divorce, the birth of a child, or significant financial shifts all warrant a review. An outdated plan is essentially no plan at all.

Take charge of your legacy. Estate planning is a profound act of love and responsibility. It's your voice, your wishes, and your values, captured in financial form, ensuring that when you're no longer here, what you've nurtured and built with care continues to support and protect the ones you hold dear. Embrace the process, and you'll craft not just wealth, but a lasting imprint on the lives of those who follow.

Teaching Kids About Money As we navigate the nuances of building generational wealth, it's essential to engage the next generation in this journey. Equipping kids with a robust financial education sets them up for success. Instilling money smarts in our young ones isn't just about teaching them to save; it's about crafting a worldview that appreciates the value of a dollar, understands the importance of financial planning, and recognizes the profound impact of fiscal responsibility.

Let's begin by appreciating that money conversations are as crucial as those heart-to-hearts about life's other big themes. Start early, and make it as natural as discussing their day at school. Young minds are impressively malleable; they absorb habits and attitudes that can last a lifetime. So, begin with the basics, like identifying coins and bills and understanding what they can buy. You can do this through board games, role-playing, and real-life shopping experiences.

As they grow, involve them in budgeting for family outings or weekly groceries. Give them a sense of agency by allowing them to make small money decisions. By giving them choices, you're empowering them with the confidence to make money decisions. This might look like deciding between ice cream flavors at the store while adhering to a budget limit—it's about evaluating choices within financial constraints.

Savings should be a thrill, not a chore. Invigorate this concept by setting up a savings jar or a piggy bank. Encourage short-term saving goals for something they really want, and celebrate when they reach their goals. This joy in achievement will seed the idea that saving can lead to rewarding experiences—a foundational belief for a healthy financial future.

As savings grow, it's time to introduce the idea of a bank account. Take your child to open their own account and involve them in the process. Help them understand what interest is and the astounding magic of compounding. It's a moment of pride for a child to see their savings earn money; it's an early lesson in passive income.

When your youngster becomes a teenager, delve into more complex topics. Budgeting their allowance or earnings from a part-time job teaches them to manage cash flow. This might also be the right moment for the 'earn, save, give' approach—allocating portions of income for spending, saving, and donating. This not only teaches money management but also instills philanthropic values.

Credit cards and loans are often the Achilles' heel for many adults. Demystify these terms for teenagers by discussing how they work, the importance of credit scores, and the dangers of falling into debt. A prepaid debit card can be a great tool to introduce these concepts, as they can practice using 'plastic' in a controlled environment without the risk of debt.

Investing should not be a taboo topic. Explain stocks and bonds in simple terms, and perhaps, let them choose a company they like to 'invest' in. You could use online simulators or real small amounts to give them a hands-on experience. The goal here is to demonstrate the idea of ownership and growth over time.

Now, let's talk entrepreneurship. If they have a business idea, support it. Whether it's a lemonade stand or a babysitting service, it's a fantastic opportunity for them to learn about profit, loss, and the grunt work that goes into earning a buck. Plus, it's a brilliant avenue for them to channel their creativity and drive.

Encourage curiosity. If they're questioning why taxes are deducted from your paycheck or how government bonds work, dive into those discussions. It's terrific that they're thinking about how the broader financial system affects personal finance. Remember, no question is too small or too silly.

Given that we're living in the digital age, it's essential to familiarize children with financial technology. Help them understand online banking, the concept of digital wallets, and the importance of cybersecurity. With the prevalence of scams and fraud, teaching them to be diligent online is just as imperative as managing money offline.

Likewise, charity and financial compassion are powerful lessons. Encourage children to set aside a portion of their money for causes they care about. This could be anything from donating to animal shelters to supporting environmental causes. It's about teaching the value of money – not just its economic worth, but its potential for positive impact in the world.

Keep the conversation ongoing and age-appropriate. As children mature, their grasp of financial concepts will deepen, and you can progressively introduce more complex ideas. Celebrate milestones — like their first paycheck or investment — and turn bumps in the road into teachable moments. Mistakes will happen; they're part of the learning curve, but with a solid foundation, they'll learn to make corrections and move forward.

In essence, teaching kids about money is about nurturing a mindset. We're not just teaching children to count money; we're empowering them to make informed decisions that align with their values and goals. We're setting the stage for a lifetime of financial independence and confidence. The habits and lessons they learn now will echo through their lives, potentially benefiting generations to come.

So, let's wrap this discussion with a promise to ourselves and the future movers and shakers of the world: make financial literacy a gift we give the young, for knowledge is the currency of choice in their tomorrow, and financial empowerment is a legacy well worth leaving behind.

Chapter 16:
Financial Technology and Tools - Embracing the Digital Age

In the high-speed world we're living in, *financial technology* has become the new black, offering chic solutions that streamline our financial lives and empower us to manage our money with confidence and clarity. Think of this digital financial revolution as your virtual money maven, a trustworthy companion in your journey toward great financial health and savvy. It's all about leveraging cutting-edge tools to make informed decisions - that means taking charge of your budget, investments, and savings plan with a few taps on your smartphone or clicks on your laptop. These tools aren't just about convenience; they're about taking control, gaining insights, and saving time so we can spend it on what truly matters. With a wealth of apps and resources at your fingertips, you'll find it easier than ever to track your spending, dive into investing without the perplexity, and even safeguard your future with automated savings strategies. So, let's embrace these tools and make them work for us, integrating this digital prowess to not just follow, but lead in the ballet of finances. And always remember, while technology is there to guide us, it's our own savvy scrutiny that ensures we remain both protected and prosperous online.

Useful Apps and Online Resources As we navigate this incredible journey toward financial fluency, it's essential to have the right tools at your fingertips. Imagine the empowerment that comes from having a suite of applications and online resources that serve as your digital financial allies. I've compiled a game-changing list of apps and online resources specifically tailored for savvy women seeking financial independence.

Firstly, budgeting apps are non-negotiable for keeping your spending in check and ensuring that you stay on track with your financial goals. Apps like Mint and You Need A Budget (YNAB) offer seamless methods for tracking your spending, categorizing expenses, and setting budget limits. They can also start to teach you about the rhythm of your cash flow - when it comes in, when it goes out, and what it's going towards.

Investing can often seem like a labyrinth of confusion. That's where tools like Robinhood and Ellevest come into the picture. Robinhood simplifies stock market investing, with zero commission fees and an intuitively designed app for beginners. Ellevest, designed with the intent to serve women investors, offers personalized investment strategies that take into account the unique career paths and life cycles of women.

Don't overlook the power of a robust retirement planning tool, such as Personal Capital. This app not only allows you to track your investments but also assesses your retirement savings, ensuring that you're on a clear path to financial security in your golden years.

Are you in the market for real estate? Apps like Zillow and Redfin can help you search for properties, estimate mortgage payments, and get a sense of the market in your desired location. Knowledge here is not just power; it's profit, too.

When it comes to tracking your debt and optimizing payments, services like Debt Payoff Planner and Unbury.Me come in handy. They allow you to visualize your debt across different accounts and create a targeted plan to tackle it effectively, whether it's via the

Avalanche method (paying off debt with the highest interest rates first) or the Snowball method (paying off the smallest debts first for psychological wins).

Saving money doesn't need to be mundane. Digit is an app that analyzes your spending habits and silently saves small amounts that you won't miss. Before you know it, you've built up a significant emergency fund or vacation stash without feeling the pinch!

One area that remains a daunting frontier for many is taxes. Thankfully, TurboTax has revolutionized the way we approach them. With its user-friendly interface, you can file your taxes with confidence, knowing you are leveraging every deduction and credit available to you.

On the topic of career growth, LinkedIn is not just for job hunting. This platform also offers a wealth of articles, courses, and networking opportunities to fuel your professional progress.

For entrepreneurial spirits looking to fund their next big venture, platforms like Kickstarter and Indiegogo offer the opportunity to crowdsource funds, while apps like Square and Stripe empower entrepreneurs to easily manage business transactions.

If you're managing finances with a partner or your family, apps like Honeydue and HomeBudget offer joint financial management tools that can sync your budgets and expenses, fostering transparency and teamwork in your financial relationship.

We all encounter moments when we need a little financial advice, and online forums like Bogleheads and Reddit's Personal Finance community can be goldmines of wisdom where you can ask questions and seek perspectives from seasoned finance enthusiasts.

To keep your financial data safe and secure, it's crucial to utilize apps with robust security measures. Look for apps with multi-factor authentication and end-to-end encryption to protect your data, such as encryption services offered by LastPass for managing your financial passwords securely.

No matter what stage of your financial journey you're on, the right tools can make all the difference in reaching your destinations with grace and confidence. These applications and online resources are not just about making transactions easier; they're about streamlining paths and building bridges to your most vibrant financial future.

This toolkit of apps and resources is a bounty for the taking. They're tailored for ease, informed by data, and, most importantly, focused on empowerment. Harness their capabilities, deepen your financial knowledge, and conquer your goals with the assurance that these digital allies are in your corner.

Imagine your financial landscape as a garden – full of potential, awaiting your care. With these tools, you're fully equipped to cultivate a garden that thrives and sustains, a haven of prosperity that's distinctly and unapologetically yours. Let's embrace these technologies with open arms and transform your financial world into one where you're the master gardener, sculpting a landscape that's not only fruitful but also a true reflection of your financial savvy and grace.

Staying Safe with Financial Technology As we glide elegantly into the digital age, managing our finances online has become as essential as having a chic wallet to store our cards. However, with this convenience comes a need for vigilance. The realm of financial technology is brimming with tools designed to simplify money management, but it's crucial to stay on your toes to protect your assets and personal information. Here's how you can use financial apps and online resources confidently, while ensuring your safety. Let's navigate this digital landscape together and keep our finances as secure as they are savvy.

First off, passwords are the guardians of your digital financial kingdom. Opt for complex, unique passwords for each financial tool you use. We know it's tempting to use your dog's name across all platforms, but resist! Also, incorporate a password manager to keep track of these passwords; it's like having a personal assistant for your digital identity.

When downloading financial apps, scrutinize their privacy policies. I don't mean a quick skim—put on your detective hat and examine what information they collect and how they vow to protect it. If the jargon seems too overwhelming, search for user reviews or ask a tech-savvy confidant. Transparency is key when it comes to whom you're trusting with your financial data.

Two-factor authentication (2FA) should be your new best friend. Whenever possible, activate this feature. Yes, it adds an extra step to logging in, but it's like throwing on a statement belt—it just makes everything more secure.

Secure Wi-Fi connections are another must. Public Wi-Fi may be convenient for quick shopping or scrolling through your feed, but it's not the place to check your bank balance. In these situations, a virtual private network (VPN) can be your hero, cloaking your online presence like the perfect trench coat on a rainy day.

Don't click on any links from unsolicited emails or messages purporting to be from a financial institution. That's an open invitation to scammers. If you're unsure, directly contact the financial institution to confirm. Think of it as confirming RSVPs to your exclusive party—better safe than sorry!

Monitor your accounts regularly. This isn't just about checking your balance; it's about being proactive in spotting any transaction that doesn't look right. Similar to reviewing your fabulous ensemble one last time before stepping out, check your financial transactions regularly to catch anything amiss. If you spot an anomaly, report it immediately.

Update, update, update! Keep your app software and mobile device up-to-date with the latest patches. These updates are like the latest fashion trends for your devices—they address vulnerabilities and keep everything running smoothly.

Take advantage of alerts and notifications set up by your financial institutions. Whether it's a text about a recent login or an email about a withdrawal, these instant updates can be as vital as a flash sale notification—immediate and cannot be missed!

Learning about common scams can help you avoid them. Stay informed about the tactics fraudsters use—it's empowering knowledge that lets you sidestep financial pitfalls with grace.

Remember, your data is valuable. Be selective about the apps you use and the information you share. Imagine your data like a limited-edition luxury item; you wouldn't just hand it out to anyone.

Backup your data regularly. Should anything happen to your device, you'll have a backup plan—consider it an insurance policy for your digital life.

Lastly, always log out from any financial site or app when you're finished using it. It's like locking the doors to your home—simple but effective.

The financial landscape may have its own set of challenges, but by employing smart, proactive strategies, you can enjoy the convenience of technology without compromising your security. It's about maintaining that balanced approach to digital finances—relishing the sophistication it brings while being uncompromising on safety. Think of these strategies as your personal protocol for financial elegance in the modern world.

By taking these security steps to heart, you can embrace financial technology with open arms, knowing that your hard-earned wealth is safeguarded with the meticulous care it deserves. After all, financial savviness isn't just about growing your wealth; it's also about protecting it with as much fervor as you would defend your signature style.

As you stride forward with financial technology as your ally, remember that staying informed, staying alert, and taking preventive measures are all hallmarks of a sophisticated financial guardian. Use these tools to your advantage, and they will empower you to thrive in the realm of digital finance, ensuring that your financial presence is as secure and radiant as you are.

Chapter 17:
Side Hustles and Startups - Extra Income Streams

Ladies, let's put the spotlight on multiplying our money moves with side hustles and startups. Imagine turning passions into paychecks and ideas into income—this chapter is your map to doing just that. Whether it's launching that Etsy store brimming with handmade jewelry or consulting based on your professional prowess, a side gig can not only pad your purse but also empower you with financial independence. At the same time, we're honing in on the ins and outs of startup culture—maybe you're envisioning the next big tech breakthrough or a cafe that becomes your town's new hotspot. We'll walk through the practical steps to transform these dreams into viable streams of income without risking your current financial stability. With an astute balance, confidence, and the savviness of a seasoned entrepreneur, you're ready to take the world by storm, one side hustle and startup at a time. Let's ignite those extra income streams and watch as they grow from a trickle into a torrent of financial progress.

Identifying Lucrative Side Gigs We've navigated the seas of setting financial goals, budgeting with finesse, and understanding how to manage debt with diva-worthy savvy. But let's zoom in on one of the most empowering steps you can take to up your financial game: identifying side gigs that don't just pad your wallet, but potentially line it with silk.

Side hustles are more than just a buzzword—they're a revolution in earning potential. Your talent, when harnessed correctly, can bloom into a profitable venture that complements your main income. Let's start with the basics: a lucrative side gig is one that offers a high return for the time you invest. It doesn't have to drain your energy like a second full-time job might. On the contrary, it should spark joy and excitement within you, serving as a platform to explore your passions and interests.

First, self-assessment is crucial. Dive deep into your skill set; what do you excel at that others might struggle with? This could be anything from graphic design, writing, or social media management, to organizing spaces or planning events. Your unique skills can morph into a service that others are willing to pay for. Consider utilizing online platforms such as Upwork or Fiverr, where freelancers thrive in a marketplace hungry for their expertise.

Don't discount your hobbies—they can be deceptively lucrative. That knitting project or jewelry making you do for fun? There's a market out there for handmade goods, and sites like Etsy are the perfect incubators for such creativity. Craftsmanship has value, so turn your pastime pleasures into a profitable pursuit.

Ever considered teaching? Online education is booming, and platforms like Teachable and Skillshare allow you to monetize your knowledge. Whether it's yoga, marketing, or web development, you can design a course and become an educator in your own right. It's about leveraging what you know and packaging it in a way that's accessible and appealing to others.

We can't overlook the local gig economy either. From ride-sharing services to food delivery, these options provide flexible work that can snugly fit around your primary job's hours. These gigs aren't just money-makers; they're networking opportunities, a chance to meet new people and often lead to unexpected opportunities.

Next, examine the scalability of potential side gigs. Freelance writing or photography can start small but evolve into a full-blown business. The key is to establish a robust portfolio and network to attract clients. Gradual expansion is not just possible, it's the template many successful entrepreneurs have used to transition from side gig to CEO.

Consider the world of beauty and wellness. If you're savvy with makeup or fitness, services such as personal training sessions or makeup consultations can be particularly profitable. With social media as a megaphone to broadcast your skills, you can build a brand that resonates with your audience and elevates your side gig to new heights.

Real estate isn't just for house-flipping TV shows—you too can get a piece of the pie by managing property or becoming an Airbnb host. With proper research and management, property can provide a steady stream of passive income, a golden goose of side hustling.

Digital products are another frontier. Write an e-book, develop an app, or create downloadable templates or art. With digital goods, production costs are minimal, and distribution can span the globe. You create once and sell infinitely—now that's a smart business model.

Remember, time is precious. Opt for side gigs that offer flexibility. There's no sense in drowning in commitments that stretch you too thin. Balance is key; your side gig should complement, not compromise, your lifestyle. It's all about finding the golden ratio of time invested to income earned.

Dipping your toes into investment as a side gig can seem daunting, but with micro-investing apps, you can start small. Invest in stocks, real estate, or other ventures with amounts that you're comfortable with. This approach can turn spare change into a growing portfolio, illustrating the power of seemingly insignificant amounts over time.

Document your side gig journey. Share your progress on a blog or social media, not only to market your services but to attract a community who'll champion your growth. Engagement builds trust, and trust converts spectators into customers and clients—paving the way for your side hustle to flourish.

Stay abreast of trends and adapt. What's in demand today may not be tomorrow. Keep learning and stay flexible, so your side gig continues to evolve just as you do. It's about being proactive, not reactive, maintaining the edge that sets you apart.

To cap it off, acknowledge that it's okay to have trial and error. Not every venture will succeed initially, and that doesn't mean failure—it means learning. Each attempt is a lesson, each setback a setup for a comeback. Your side hustle could be a stepping stone to your next adventure in financial empowerment.

Never forget that these endeavors are not just about making extra cash; they're about creating a richer life experience—one where you're in the driver's seat, mastering your own financial destiny.

Balancing Side Hustles with Full-Time Work As we dive into blending the zest of side hustles with the commitment of full-time work, it's essential to underline just how empowering this balancing act can be. Not only can a side gig fuel your financial goals, but it can also stoke the fires of your passions and creativity. However, the challenge remains: orchestrating this symphony of productivity without missing a beat.

First, let's talk time management. You have the same 24 hours in a day as everyone else, and how you spend them can be a game-changer. Prioritizing is key. Assess your side hustle activities and ask yourself what can be streamlined, what requires your immediate attention, and what can wait. And remember, sometimes the most productive thing you can do is take a breather. Rest isn't a luxury; it's essential for keeping you at the top of your game.

Speaking of rest, burning the candle at both ends isn't sustainable. Your health and well-being should always come first. If your side hustle starts to undermine your quality of life or your performance at your day job, it's time to reassess. Setting boundaries will help safeguard your energy and ensure that your side endeavor enhances, rather than diminishes, your life.

Communication is another cornerstone of balancing these worlds. If you're employed, being upfront with your employer about your side hustle can help manage expectations on both sides. Transparency builds trust, and you'll appreciate having your employer in your corner when you need a more flexible schedule.

Efficiency is your ally. Automate whatever tasks you can in your side hustle to save time and reduce manual efforts. Whether it's scheduling social media posts or handling invoicing, let technology take some of the burdens off your shoulders.

Don't be afraid to invest in your side hustle, too. This could mean outsourcing tasks that aren't in your wheelhouse or that take too much of your time. Time is often more valuable than money, and paying for expert help can free you up to focus on areas where you excel.

Networking isn't just for job hunters; it's a lifeline for the side hustler. Surrounding yourself with a supportive community can lead to shared resources, advice, and possibly even collaborative opportunities. All of which can amplify the success of your side hustle with less direct time investment from you.

Understanding the ebb and flow of productivity during the day is crucial. Are you a morning person or a night owl? Harnessing the times when you're most alert and energetic can make your hustle more enjoyable and productive. Aligning your side hustle work with your natural rhythms can lead to better outcomes and less stress.

It's important to keep your eyes on the financial prize, too. As you juggle your full-time job and side hustle, ensure you're tracking your income and expenses meticulously. This financial clarity not only guides your efforts but also prepares you for tax time, which can be more complex with multiple streams of income.

Goal setting isn't just for your full-time career. Establishing clear, targeted goals for your side hustle will help you maintain focus and measure progress. And these goals should align with your overall financial plan, ensuring that your side gig is moving you towards your vision of financial freedom.

Let's not forget about your legal and financial responsibilities. It's critical to understand any potential conflicts of interest and to respect any non-compete clauses with your full-time employer. Diligence in these areas safeguards your reputation and your primary source of income.

Further, make learning a part of your routine. Staying informed about best practices in both your full-time work and side hustle can open doors to efficiencies and opportunities you might not have considered. Knowledge truly is power, and it's a currency that's always in your control.

Pacing is everything. While it's tempting to go all-in on your side hustle, especially when things are going well, remember that you're in this for the long haul. Sustainable growth often requires a slow and steady approach, which is especially true when balancing it with a full-time job.

In the event that your side hustle starts to outshine your day job in potential and passion, it might be time to consider a shift. That transition will be smoother if you've maintained professionalism and performance in your full-time role. In other words, excel at your job until you're ready to make your hustle your main gig, and that choice will be yours to make organically.

Lastly, maintain a mindset of flexibility and a heart centered on why you started your side hustle in the first place. Keep revisiting and, if necessary, redefining what success looks like for you. Sometimes the greatest victories are not in the numbers but in the confidence and self-reliance you build along the way. Your side hustle paired with your career is not just about making ends meet; it's about weaving a rich tapestry of experience and wealth that is all your own.

Keep these strategies in mind as we head into creating additional income streams, and remember that balance isn't static—it's a constant, dynamic process. With focus, resilience, and a savvy approach, you can wear both your professional career and side hustle like the complementary accessories they are, accentuating your financial independence and personal satisfaction.

Chapter 18:
Global Glam - International
Investing and Diversification

Imagine stretching your financial wings to glide over a mosaic of global markets, where opportunity dances to the rhythm of different currencies and cultures. Expanding our portfolios beyond our borders isn't just about adding a touch of exotic flair—it's a savvy move to diversify and potentially boost our financial health. As world economies ebb and flow, you're not just protecting your hard-earned wealth; you're embracing a world of new possibilities. Dipping into international waters can be as thrilling as finding that perfect pair of shoes on sale in a foreign boutique—it's all about knowing where to look and the right fit for your financial wardrobe. Whether you're eyeing the vibrant energy of emerging markets or considering the stable stride of established economies, stepping into global investing can help balance your investment portfolio and mitigate the risks tied to any single market. Remember, while trends come and go, diversification is always in vogue. So, let's twirl across the globe together and discover how international investing can be your runway to financial resilience and elegance. After all, in the world of finance, diversity isn't just chic—it's essential.

Exploring Emerging Markets As we've navigated through investments closer to our own backyard, it's time to dress our portfolios with a bit of international flair. Consider this: Emerging markets. These are like the vibrant, bold prints that catch your eye in a boutique window, a little intimidating at first but potentially transformative for your wardrobe—or in this case, your investment strategy.

Now, 'emerging markets' is a term that brings with it visions of countries like Brazil, Russia, India, China, and South Africa, also known as the BRICS nations. They're like the new kids on the economic block—young, energetic, possibly unpredictable, but brimming with potential. They're the economies in transition, aiming to move from developing to developed status, much like a tech startup yearning to become the next unicorn.

Investing in these markets means tapping into their growth. Yes, there are risks—markets can be volatile, political instability is real, and there's the currency quagmire to wade through. But isn't it thrilling? The rewards can be substantial when you get it right. It's a bit like landing the perfect job offer; it takes preparation and timing, but the payoff is career acceleration.

Understanding the unique nature of these economies is vital. They often have young populations, increasing consumerism, and rapid technological adoption. Think of them as social media influencers—trendsetters who could lead the next wave of economic trends. And for you, my intelligent ally in finance, this could mean a golden opportunity to diversify and potentially boost returns.

Before diving into emerging market investments, equip yourself with knowledge about the political, economic, and social landscapes of the countries you're interested in. It's like meeting a partner's parents for the first time—you want to know what you're getting into and understand the family dynamics.

One exciting way to invest in these economies is through emerging market funds or ETFs. They're akin to a curated collection from a boutique—you get a variety of pieces that can bring your outfit, or in this case, your portfolio, to life. The diversification within these funds can help mitigate some of the risks these markets present.

Don't overlook the significance of currency risks. When you invest internationally, fluctuations in currency can affect the value of your investments. Imagine planning a luxury vacation abroad, and suddenly the currency exchange rates take an unexpected turn—your beautifully planned budget can take a hit. The same applies to your investments.

Corporate governance is another aspect that can't be ignored. These markets can have different rules when it comes to company transparency and shareholder rights. It's like checking a designer's ethical practices before splurging on their line; due diligence goes a long way in ensuring you're making informed decisions.

Are you worried about risk? It's a natural feeling. But remember, with a proper strategy, you can navigate these waters. Starting small and using only a portion of your portfolio for emerging markets can be a wise move. It's like trying a new health regimen; you start with small, measurable steps to gauge how your body responds.

Inflation and commodity prices can significantly impact emerging markets—different from developed nations. Learning about the commodity cycle is like understanding why certain fabrics are more expensive during different seasons. This knowledge can inform when you should invest, adding another layer of sophistication to your financial insights.

Consider working with a financial advisor with international investment experience. That's your stylist for the global economic runway—a guide who can help tailor your investment choices to your risk tolerance, financial goals, and personal style.

Stay informed about global events. When you understand world news and its implications, you can anticipate market movements. It's the equivalent of being a trend-spotter in fashion; you know what's coming and can prepare your closet, or in this case, your portfolio, accordingly.

Socially responsible investing can also come into play here. As you seek to add emerging market flair, consider companies and funds committed to positive social and environmental impacts. Think of this as shopping with a conscience—you know your money is not just earning returns but making a difference.

As women forging our path in finance, exploring emerging markets isn't just about growing wealth—it's about participating in and influencing the global economy. These markets offer a window into the future, a chance to partake in the growth stories that will shape our world.

So, let's not shy away from this exciting journey. With careful research, professional advice, and a diverse approach, emerging markets can be a strikingly chic addition to your portfolio. Remember, every bold move can bring distinct vibrancy to your financial independence.

In our next chapter, we'll gracefully sidestep potential pitfalls by 'Managing Currency Risk.' This will equip you further to be a global investor, balancing the scales of risk and reward—key to mastering the art of international investment diversity. Let's continue to weave the stunning tapestry of our financial futures, one thread of wisdom at a time.

Managing Currency Risk Let's delve into the world of international investing, a realm where opportunities for growth are as vibrant and varied as the cultures that give them life. But with these opportunities come risks, and one of the sneakiest players on this field is currency risk. Understanding how to manage currency risk isn't just smart investing; it's a power move towards financial sovereignty.

Now, imagine you're taking a beautiful international tapestry and adding it to your investment collection. Just as the patterns and colors of the tapestry reflect different aspects of the culture from which they originate, your international investments reflect a diverse array of economic climates. But here's the catch: as currencies fluctuate in value against your own, they can affect the real return of your investment. We don't want that, do we?

To start, currency risk, also known as exchange-rate risk, occurs when the value of your foreign investment changes due to fluctuating exchange rates. Say you've invested in a shiny new European stock, and it performs splendidly. But when you convert your Euros back to Dollars, you find that the Euro has weakened against the Dollar. Frustratingly, this can erode your gains or even turn them into losses. That's what we're here to avoid.

Now, how do we tackle this unwelcome guest? First, consider currency-hedged funds. These are mutual funds or ETFs that use sophisticated strategies to neutralize currency risk. They're like having an elegant shawl to drape over that tapestry, shielding it from the unpredictable weather of currency fluctuations.

Another savvy move is to diversify your currency exposure. Put your chips in different pots, so to speak. By spreading your investments across various currencies, a dip in one might be balanced out by a rise in another. It's about not keeping all your eggs in one currency basket, diversifying within diversification. It's financial elegance at its finest.

You might also want to consider using stop-loss orders. Setting a stop-loss is like instructing your investments to strut out of the door if the party turns sour. This helps you sell off your foreign assets if the currency exchange rate starts to plummet and reach your pre-set point, potentially protecting you from deeper losses.

Understanding macroeconomic factors can also grant you an edge. Factors such as inflation rates, monetary policies, and political stability can drastically influence currency values. Keep a sharp eye on these indicators. It's like continuously assessing the wind's direction when sailing; you want to navigate the economic seas wisely.

Also, weigh the merits of investing in stable, well-established currencies versus volatile, high-growth ones. Strong currencies may offer less growth potential but come with fewer rollercoaster rides. Emerging market currencies could pack a punch in terms of growth, but volatility can be high. Think of it as choosing between a reliable sedan and a zippy sports car, each has its time and place.

Forward contracts can also protect you from currency risk. These financial instruments allow you to lock in a currency exchange rate for future transactions. It's a promise between you and the currency market, where you agree to exchange at a specified rate, no matter which way the market winds blow.

When engaging in international investing, keeping an eye on currency trends can't be overstated. Trends often signal broader economic shifts, and catching these can help you adjust your portfolio in a proactive fashion. Like fashion trends, you don't need to follow them blindly, but being aware is critical.

Automating some of these protective strategies can also ease the burden of managing currency risk. Various financial platforms can monitor exchange rates and execute defensive measures when certain criteria are met. It's like having your own personal financial bodyguard keeping tabs on your assets.

Remember, managing currency risk involves both strategic decisions and a mindset shift. You're not merely an investor; you're a global financial connoisseur. Appreciate the nuances and embrace the complexities. It's part of the rich, empowering journey of international investing.

Finally, just as you seek professional advice for fashion, don't shy away from consulting financial experts specialized in currency markets. Their insights can add a layer of sophistication to your international investment strategy. It's like personal shopping for your portfolio, bringing in expertise to enhance your choices.

In sum, managing currency risk is like adding an essential accessory to your financial ensemble. It requires attentiveness, flexibility, and a touch of finesse. Take the time to explore which methods align with your investment style and financial goals. With the right strategies, you can tiptoe through the currency minefield with grace and emerge on the other side, not just unscathed, but flourishing.

And there you have it, a mosaic of strategies to manage currency risk. Don't let the fear of fluctuating currencies hold you back from painting your investment portfolio with international colors. After all, financial independence is about painting your own masterpiece, full of risks you understand and rewards you've gracefully secured. Go ahead, embrace those global opportunities, and weave them into your financial future with confidence and poise.

Chapter 19:
Cryptocurrency Couture -
Decoding Digital Currencies

In the fast-paced world of finance, unearthing the mysteries of digital currencies often feels like translating an exotic language—intimidating at first, but empowering once you've got the hang of it. As we weave through the vibrant tapestry of cryptocurrency, it's time to unravel the threads that make up this intricate domain. Imagine strolling through the digital marketplace—each coin a unique stitch in the fabric of this online economy. We're not just talking about Bitcoin here; there's a whole fashion show of options gliding down the runway. But let's be real, the volatility of these digital assets can be as unpredictable as the hemline trends in fashion week. So, rather than jumping on every 'trendy' crypto that struts by, let's gain insights into the robust blockchain technology and understand its potential to transform not just how we view currency, but also the very bedrock of our financial transactions. Embrace the confidence to ask the tough questions: What does cryptocurrency mean for your wallet? Is it the right fit for your financial portfolio—or should you leave it to those with a penchant for digital daring? With each step in this chapter, you'll come closer to mastering the elegance of cryptocurrency, wrapping yourself in newfound knowledge that not only looks good but makes practical, fiscal sense, too.

Bitcoin and Blockchain Basics Now, as we're rapidly moving through an age where technology reinvents the way we handle money, it's crucial for us to demystify some of the jargon and concepts that are reshaping the financial landscape. Enter the world of Bitcoin and blockchain - terms that might sound like they're straight out of a sci-fi novel, but in reality, they're knocking on the doorsteps of our everyday transactions.

Let's start with the heart of it all: blockchain. Think of it as a digital ledger that's completely open to anyone. It records transactions in a secure and transparent manner. Each "block" is like a page of this ledger, filled with a list of transactions. Once a block is filled, it's linked to the previous block, forming a chain - hence the name, blockchain.

Bitcoin, on the other hand, is a type of cryptocurrency which means it's a digital currency that operates independently of any central bank or government. It's like the gold standard for the digital age. Bitcoin runs on a blockchain platform, ensuring that every transaction is recorded in a manner that's almost impossible to tamper with. It's a currency that gives power to the people, sidestepping the traditional financial power structures.

Think of when you make a digital payment and it goes through various checks and balances – that's the bank's infrastructure at work. With Bitcoin, the blockchain replaces those middlemen. It's decentralized; its infrastructure is maintained by a network of computers, operated by individuals all over the world, known as miners. They verify and record transactions into new blocks in the blockchain and in return, they're rewarded with Bitcoin.

Now you might wonder, how does one own Bitcoin? You can either purchase it through various exchanges, or you can earn it through mining, which involves using computer power to solve complex mathematical puzzles that maintain the blockchain. Owning Bitcoin means having a digital wallet, which is like an online bank account specifically for your cryptocurrency. From there, you can send, receive, and manage your Bitcoin.

The allure of Bitcoin doesn't stop at its novelty; it's also become an investment asset, much like stocks and gold. Its value can be quite volatile, swinging up and down in response to market demands, world events, and investor sentiment. This can make it an exciting, albeit risky, addition to a portfolio.

One of the biggest questions with Bitcoin and blockchain is - how secure are they? The blockchain is designed with cryptography, making it secure by default. As long as you keep your wallet's private key inaccessible to others, your Bitcoins are safe. However, as with all things tech, it's essential to stay updated on security practices. It's uncharted territory, and where there's value, there are also those attempting to exploit vulnerabilities.

Another hot topic is the anonymity factor. Unlike your bank account, Bitcoin and blockchain offer a level of anonymity because transactions are tied to wallet IDs, not your personal details. That's wonderfully liberating for privacy advocates but has also raised concerns about potential uses in illegal activities. It's a digital double-edged sword; empowering yet demanding caution and responsibility.

Immersion in blockchain and Bitcoin doesn't require a tech background – understanding their principles and implications is enough to get you started. They represent a democratisation of financial security and efficiency, cutting across socioeconomic boundaries and enabling a global inclusiveness that's quite revolutionary.

Furthermore, learning about Bitcoin could offer you opportunities beyond simple transactions. As investors seek to diversify and protect their assets against inflation and market uncertainties, Bitcoin presents itself as an alternative investment. You're not just putting money in an account; you're stepping into an arena where you can potentially grow your wealth in ways that traditional currency can't offer.

The technologies fueling Bitcoin and blockchain are constantly evolving, and staying abreast of them is much like keeping up with the latest fashion trends - it's an ongoing process. Embrace the learning curve, get comfortable with the basics, and you might just find yourself ahead of the curve.

However, don't let the buzz around Bitcoin sweep you into making impulsive investment decisions. Just because it's trending doesn't mean it should throw your financial goals off track. If you consider dipping your toes in this digital currency pond, do it with diligence, research, and perhaps even seek advice from a financial advisor who understands the space.

Remember, as with all investing, there's no guarantee of returns with Bitcoin, and it should be viewed as part of a broader, diversified investment strategy. It's about striking a balance; leveraging the exciting potential of Bitcoin while maintaining the financial foundations we've built up to this point in our journey.

Bitcoin and blockchain are more than just buzzwords; they're portals to understanding how technology intersects with our financial wellbeing. They encourage us to ask questions, seek answers, and remain both curious and cautious as we navigate through the digital economy. As we continue to explore the diverse aspects of feminine finance, let's keep the spirit of innovation alive, alongside the wisdom of prudent financial management.

Many of you may be asking, "Is Bitcoin something I should include in my financial plans?" As we peek into the next section, we'll delve into this question and weigh the potential risks and rewards of integrating cryptocurrency into your investment portfolio. It's all about informed choice and aligning investments with your unique financial goals and comfort levels.

Should You Invest in Cryptocurrency? Continuing our journey through the myriad of investment choices, let's unravel the enigma of cryptocurrency. Amidst the cacophony of contemporary investment avenues, cryptocurrencies have emerged as a polarizing and yet intriguing player. You've probably heard the buzz around Bitcoin, Ethereum, and perhaps the allure of prospective riches that they could hold. But the million-dollar question remains: Should you channel your hard-earned money into this digital currency universe?

First things first, investing isn't a one-size-fits-all game. Just like we pick the right shoes for an occasion, we must select investments that complement our financial objectives and risk appetite. Cryptocurrency's volatility is notorious, with prices swinging wildly in short periods. That could mean the potential for high returns, but likewise, the risk of steep losses. Can you stay poised if your investment's value fluctuates dramatically?

Here's what's captivating about cryptocurrency: it's decentralized nature. Unlike traditional currency, crypto isn't controlled by any single government or institution, offering a sense of financial freedom that's empowering. It's an assertion of autonomy - but with great power comes great responsibility. Understanding the blockchain technology that underpins crypto is crucial. Lack of knowledge could lead to your downfall in this complex domain.

Think of crypto like the edgy, high-fashion item in your wardrobe - exciting, perhaps groundbreaking, but also unpredictable. It should never make up the entirety of your investment ensemble. Prudent investing calls for diversification. Your portfolio should be a tapestry of different assets, providing balance and protection against market swings.

Remember, there's no rewind button in investing. If you decide to take the plunge into crypto, start small. Just as you wouldn't pour your entire budget into a single pair of designer shoes, don't allocate a disproportionate slice of your investment pie to crypto. Consider it as an experimental addition – only what you can afford to lose without it impacting your financial stability.

Discussions about cryptocurrency are often peppered with stories of overnight millionaires. But for every rags-to-riches anecdote, there are untold stories of those who have lost significantly. Investment decisions should never be made on the whims of FOMO (Fear of Missing Out). Instead, they should be grounded in research, an understanding of market dynamics, and an assessment of one's financial threshold for risk.

While traditional investments like stocks and bonds have historical data to draw on, predicting cryptocurrency's trajectory is like attempting to forecast the next fashion trend: thrilling and speculative. Are you game for speculation, or do you prefer the tried-and-true consistency of established markets?

Then there's the tax aspect. Unlike stock dividends and bond interest, which have clear tax guidelines, the tax implications of cryptocurrency earnings can be murky and, depending on your locale, could present added layers of complexity. Staying above board with the IRS requires diligent record-keeping and an understanding of the tax impacts of your crypto investments.

Security is another facet to consider. Cryptocurrency falls prey to cyber threats more than traditional investments do. Your digital wallet, much like a designer clutch, needs safeguarding. Are you prepared to navigate the security protocols essential to protect your cryptos, such as two-factor authentication and cold storage options? It's like protecting your treasures in a vault as opposed to under your mattress.

For those with an adventurous spirit, cryptocurrency could be a thrilling excursion into the future of money. But it demands you stay informed and agile. It's a fluid landscape that can reshape itself overnight, with regulations and technologies evolving at a breakneck pace. The learning curve is steep, and staying educated is non-negotiable.

If you're drawn to the potential societal impact of cryptocurrency, there's more to ponder. Advocates hail crypto as a democratizing force in finance, opening doors for individuals around the world who don't have access to traditional banking. When investing, consider not just the potential gains for yourself, but also the broader implications your investment holds.

Ask yourself, do you have the time and interest to monitor your investment regularly? Unlike more passive investments that can flourish with periodic check-ins, investing in cryptocurrency often necessitates a more hands-on approach. Market trends, new coins, regulatory news - all can affect your investment in real-time.

Perhaps you're an entrepreneurial spirit, intrigued by the opportunities crypto offers beyond mere currency - like smart contracts and non-fungible tokens (NFTs). These reflect not just an investment in digital coins, but in the technology that could underpin future commerce and digital interactions.

Tapping into cryptocurrency could be invigorating, sparking a passion for learning about the digital economy's frontier. If you're the type of person who thrives on pioneering into new territories and is financially equipped to embrace volatility with poise, crypto might be the investment spice your portfolio could handle.

Ultimately, whether or not you should invest in cryptocurrency is about aligning with your financial goals and risk tolerance. It's about asking yourself if you're prepared to walk this path, armed with knowledge and a robust sense of what you stand to gain - and perhaps lose. Just like high fashion, it's not for everyone, but for some, it could be the touch that makes the outfit shine.

Chapter 20:
Financial Feminism -
Advocating for Equality

As we turn the page to Chapter 20, let's get fired up about something that's not just a cause, but a crusade for change: Financial Feminism. Here's where we stand up against the disparities dragging us down, from the gender pay gap to the investment chasm that separates us from our male counterparts. This chapter isn't just about shining a light on the inequalities—it's a rallying cry to arm yourself with knowledge, to empower every woman with the financial know-how to not merely survive, but thrive. Together, we'll explore why your investments are your voice in the financial world and how, through education and advocacy, we can collectively work towards a level playing field. Financial feminism isn't just about individual success; it's about lifting each other up, ensuring every woman has the tools to build a future that's not only prosperous but downright resplendent. So let's dive in and turn finance into our most powerful platform for equality.

The Gender Pay Gap and Investment Disparity The gender pay gap has long been a point of contention and a palpable barrier against women's financial empowerment. The numbers don't lie: on average, women earn less than men. But this isn't just a matter of salaries. The ripple effects extend far beyond take-home pay - they touch on how women invest, the risks they're willing to take, and the long-term accumulation of wealth.

Across the board, women face unique challenges when it comes to investing. Historically, we've been left out of conversations about money, leading to gaps in financial literacy. And let's face it, even in today's times, the financial world can feel like it's sporting a 'boys' club' sign. It can be intimidating, but here's the kicker: When women do invest, they often outperform men because they tend to take a long-term, calculated approach.

Now, let's talk about some cold hard cash - or rather, the lack thereof. One of the most glaring outcomes of earning less is having less money to invest. Compound this with breaks in one's career to care for family, and the problem amplifies. Less money in the market means less growth, and over time, a significant disparity in wealth between genders emerges.

Despite these hurdles, there is hope yet. The investment landscape is changing, and a more diverse array of options makes it easier for women to jump into investing. We aren't destined to let the gender pay gap define our financial futures. With the right strategies, we can narrow, if not close, that investment gap.

First, let's focus on empowering ourselves with knowledge. Understanding the basics of investment - stocks, bonds, retirement accounts, real estate - is non-negotiable. Let's become fluent in the language of investing; after all, you wouldn't go to a foreign country without learning a few key phrases, right?

Education leads to confidence, and confidence equips us to ask the right questions and make informed decisions. We can't rely on anyone else to secure our financial future. It's time to take the reins and do it ourselves.

Next up is setting financial goals, despite earning disparities. Smart investment isn't necessarily about huge lump sums; it's also about consistency. Automatic monthly contributions to a retirement account or investment fund can lead to substantial growth over time, thanks to compound interest.

There's also a cultural shift that needs to happen regarding women and money. Talking openly about finances, sharing resources, and celebrating financial wins - big or small - can help to destigmatize the conversation around women's wealth.

Then there's the importance of negotiation. Many women shy away from negotiations, which can start the pay gap cycle from the get-go. By honing this skill, you ensure you're not leaving money on the table, money that could otherwise be growing in an investment account.

And who says you have to go at it alone? Investing clubs and online communities offer support, insights, and encouragement. They offer safe spaces to learn and grow together. Strength, after all, comes in numbers.

Additionally, women should consider speaking to a financial advisor. A professional can help craft a personalized investment strategy that accounts for the realities of the gender pay gap while maximizing potential returns.

Bearing in mind these strategies is crucial because investment disparity doesn't just affect our bank accounts; it affects our dreams, our choices, and our futures. Shedding light on it is not about playing the victim; it's about becoming victorious over our circumstances. It's about taking control of what's rightfully ours: financial security and independence.

Investing isn't just about wealth; it's about wielding power over your own life. It's about not depending on a partner, a family member, or the government for financial security. It's about having the freedom to make choices that align with your personal values and lifestyle.

Lastly, throw out the outdated manual that says investing is not for women. It's 2023, and it's time for a new narrative. We can and will conquer the financial barriers that stand before us – with grace in our step and a portfolio in our hands.

So, as we move ahead in this journey, let's pledge to take active control over our financial destinies. It's not just about closing the gender gap—it's about opening up a world of possibilities where our ambitions are as limitless as our potential to achieve them. Let's invest not just in stocks and bonds, but in ourselves, our know-how, and our unwavering resolve to rise above disparity and towards financial triumph.

Empowering Women through Financial Education As we weave through the rich tapestry of financial concepts and strategies, let's turn the spotlight on a game-changer: financial education for women. It's no secret that knowledge is power, and when it comes to navigating the financial seas, education is the compass. We know all too well how historically, financial discourse has been dominated by men. Well, the winds of change are blowing, and it's high time to hoist our sails and catch it full-on.

Ladies, let's tackle the truth head-on: money matters. Understanding the how's and why's of personal finance isn't just advantageous; it's essential. Why? Because financial confidence doesn't just change your bank balance - it transforms your life, your choices, and your future. It's about walking into a room with the certainty that you're the master of your fiscal fate.

So what does it mean to be financially educated? Simply put, it's about having the knowledge to make informed decisions about all things dough-related. Sounds daunting? It's not. Not when you approach learning with the same blend of curiosity and determination that you bring to every area of your life.

Financial literacy doesn't mean you need to be a stock market wizard or the next finance guru. No, it's about understanding the basics - the kind of stuff that affects daily life. Budgeting, saving, investing, negotiating a raise - these shouldn't be skills tucked away for the elite; they're the nitty-gritty, day-to-day tools that can ensure we're not just surviving, but thriving.

Take budgeting, for example. Old-fashioned? Hardly. Creating a budget is your declaration of independence. It's a declaration that you're in control, that you know where your money's going, and more importantly, why. And saving? It's not just about stashing cash for a rainy day. It's about giving your future self the gift of security and options.

Now let's talk about the unsung hero of financial empowerment: investing. Investment isn't a boys' club anymore; it's a space where women are increasingly carving out their ground. By understanding the basics of investing, you're building a ladder to financial highs previously out of reach.

But it's not just about making money – it's also about keeping it. Debt management is critical. Knowing the difference between debilitating debt and leveraging loans to your advantage can make or break your financial health. As women, being savvy about debt means we can elevate our credit scores, enjoy financial security, and access opportunities that enable us to live abundantly.

And yes, the landscape of finance is traditionally complex. But guess what? It's nothing you can't handle. Benefits, retirement accounts, insurance – they're all pieces of the puzzle that you, with a bit of knowledge, can perfectly place. Think about retirement planning as planting a garden – what you sow today, you'll reap in spades when you're ready to bask in the sun of your golden years.

Let's not overlook the professional sphere, either. Negotiating salaries, understanding promotions, and career growth are all facets of financial education. Why? Because your income is the engine of your financial vehicle. Knowing how to rev that engine is how you'll speed ahead, leaving inequalities in the dust.

Remember, financial education is not one-size-fits-all. The beauty of this journey is its capacity for personalization. What works for you may not work for someone else, and vice versa. Have you considered starting your own business? Unlocking the potential of entrepreneurship is yet another avenue where financial literacy shines, paving the way to economic autonomy.

No conversation about financial education is complete without a nod to taxes and tax planning. They might not be the spice of life, but understanding them sure as heck can spice up your bank account. Play your cards right with deductions and credits, and tax season becomes less of a nightmare and more of a windfall.

Let's also focus on one of the most gloriously complex aspects of finance: investments and the stock market. By demystifying these arenas, we arm ourselves with the ability to grow wealth far beyond our regular income. It's about watching your hard-earned dollars work even harder for you.

Now, with all this talk about empowerment, let's not forget the role technology plays. With fintech innovations at our fingertips, managing our finances is easier than ever. And the savvy use of tech is not just convenient - it's empowering. It's about staying on top of your financial game no matter where you are or what you're doing.

So how do we get there? How do we turn the key in the ignition of our financial vehicle? It starts with education – with resources, workshops, books, and perhaps most importantly, conversations.

Money talk can no longer be taboo among us. Sharing knowledge and experiences isn't just helpful; it's revolutionary.

And while we're at it, let's forge a sisterhood of financial savvy. There's strength in numbers, and where one woman thrives, she sets the stage for others to follow. Let's mentor, guide, and uplift each other. Let's celebrate each win, whether it's mastering the art of budgeting or making a smart investment choice.

Embracing financial education is akin to grabbing your life by the horns – it's your roar of independence, your battle cry against uncertainty. And yes, it's about building wealth, but more so, it's about crafting a life full of choice and opportunity. Education breeds confidence, and with confidence comes control; and when you have control, well, that's when the magic happens.

In this chapter, we might not be diving into the gritty details of specific financial strategies – that's the delicious fare of the chapters to come. But the cornerstone of all that advice? Education. So let's commit to that first empowering step: to learn, to grow, and to flourish financially – not just for ourselves, but for our daughters, sisters, and the incredible lineage of women to come.

Chapter 21:
Mindful Money - Emotional
Spending and Financial Self-Care

We've just delved into how to standing up for fiscal equality can revamp not only our own lives, but society as a whole. Now let's switch gears and focus inward—on the often-overlooked intersection of emotional wellness and financial habits. When it comes to money, it's easy to let feelings drive our spending, leading us down a path of buyer's remorse and budgetary chaos. In this chapter, we're putting emotional spending under a microscope, unraveling the threads that lead to impulsive purchases and the stress that often follows. We'll walk through discovering your emotional spending triggers—those moments when you're tempted to treat yourself to a little retail therapy to soothe stress, celebrate, or combat boredom. Then, we're going to unwrap practical, empowering strategies to rewire your spending reflexes, replacing the rush of impulse buys with the serenity of financial self-care. We're talking about creating a money mindfulness practice that aligns your spending with your deepest values and long-term financial targets. Empower yourself by recognizing that spending can be both a source of joy and a carefully chosen tool to build the life you envision. Let's master the fine art of mindful spending together, transforming our relationship with money into one of intentional, purposeful engagement.

Recognizing Emotional Spending Triggers So you've been introduced to the basics of budgeting and the thrill of setting SMART financial goals. Let's pivot to an equally crucial, though often less-discussed, aspect of financial well-being: emotional spending triggers. They're the sneaky signals prompting you to pull out your wallet when emotions, not logic, take the helm.

Now, we've all been there. You have a rough day at work, and suddenly, a shiny new pair of shoes begins whispering your name. Or maybe it's that designer bag you've been eyeing that now seems like a 'must-have' to lift your spirits. It's these moments we need to pause and get to know the triggers that lead us down a costly path.

Firstly, let's tackle stress. It's a common trigger, and it loves company. When stress levels rise, your willpower tends to drop, making it easier to justify impulsive purchases. Be mindful that after a long, tiring day, your defenses are down, and retail therapy might seem like the perfect cure, but it's often a temporary fix.

Sadness is another trigger. If you're feeling down, it's natural to seek a quick pick-me-up. Retailers know this and target emotional marketing campaigns to make you believe that buying something equals happiness. Remember, this happiness is usually fleeting. Instead, seek out healthier avenues to address your emotions, like talking to a friend or going for a walk.

Boredom can lead to unnecessary spending as well. With a few swipes on your phone, you can fill your online shopping cart, not out of need, but merely to pass the time. Recognize this pattern; find hobbies or activities that enrich your soul without draining your wallet.

Peer pressure isn't just a thing for teenagers. Social influences can prod you into spending on experiences or items to maintain a certain image or keep up with friends. Stand firm in your financial identity and don't let FOMO (fear of missing out) dictate your spending habits.

Celebrations and rewards can be tricky. It's important to celebrate achievements, but if every success comes with a pricey reward, it's time to rethink how you celebrate. Can you swap out a shopping spree for something less costly but equally rewarding?

Festival seasons and holidays are potential landmines for emotional spending. The spirit of the season can lead to a loosening of purse strings under the guise of generosity. Set a festive budget in advance to keep your spending in check during these times.

Even positive emotions, such as excitement or love, can trigger overindulgence. It's wonderful to be in high spirits, but that doesn't mean your spending should soar too. Keep your emotions from dictating your spending by sticking to a plan.

Understanding triggers is the first step, but let's talk about how to manage them. Awareness is critical. When you can anticipate and recognize these triggers, you place yourself in a position of power. You start to distinguish between want and need, between emotional comfort and financial sense.

Create a buffer between the trigger and action. When the urge to splurge hits, hit pause. Wait it out. Give yourself a 24-hour rule, especially for big-ticket items. Often, the desire wanes, and you're grateful for not giving in.

Know your stress-relief strategies that don't involve your wallet. Whether it's meditation, exercise, or a creative outlet, have alternatives that offer you comfort and decompression without a cost.

Enlist your support system. Friends or family members who understand your financial aspirations can offer encouragement and accountability when you're tempted to make emotion-driven purchases.

Regularly review your financial goals. This action serves as a reminder of what you're working towards and helps to put impulsive spending into perspective. Is this purchase moving you closer to your goals, or is it a detour?

Track your spending. You can use an app, spreadsheet, or old-fashioned pen and paper. Seeing where your money goes can sometimes be the reality check needed to curb emotional spending.

Last but certainly not least, forgive yourself if you slip up. We're all human, and mistakes happen. Learn from the experience and strengthen your strategy to resist future triggers.

Recognizing and managing emotional spending triggers plays a substantial role in securing financial independence. Implementing these strategies won't just influence your bank balance; they'll fortify your emotional resilience — a priceless asset on your journey to financial savvy and success.

Tips for Mindful Spending Practices Mindful spending isn't just about cutting coupons and denying yourself the latte. It's a holistic approach to understanding where your money goes, and most importantly, ensuring it's aligned with your values and financial goals. Here are some chic strategies to hone your spending habits without sacrificing your style or happiness.

Firstly, begin with introspection. Ask yourself, why are you buying what you're buying? Is it out of necessity, pleasure, or perhaps social pressures? Awareness is the first step towards change, and identifying your motives can help curb impulsive purchases.

Let's take a breath and consider wants versus needs. A need is something that's essential for your survival and well-being, while a want is something that can enhance your life. By clearly differentiating the two, you can allocate your resources more effectively.

Embrace the art of waiting. Sometimes that dress on the display might seem like a must-have, but give it a week. If it's still calling your name, assess if it's within your budget. This pause can help diminish fleeting urges and focus on items that bring lasting joy.

Allocate funds for fun, because self-care is not selfish. Set aside a portion of your budget for treats and leisure. Life's too short for constant restriction, and you're more likely to stick to your financial plan if it includes a little sparkle.

When it comes to shopping, list-making is your high-fashion accessory. Walk into the store (or browse online) with a clear shopping list and stick to it. This small act of preparation can prevent whimsical spending on items you might later regret.

Adopt the use of cash or a debit card for daily expenses instead of a credit card. The tangibility of cash leaving your wallet can make you more conscious of your spending. With a debit card, you'll feel the direct impact on your bank balance.

It's also wise to track your spending. Whether it's a smartphone app or an old-fashioned ledger, recording your transactions can reveal patterns you may want to adjust. Knowledge is power, and when you're aware of where your money goes, you can redirect it to where you want it to go.

Reflect on the power of quality over quantity. Investing in a well-crafted piece that will last years can be more satisfying and economical than purchasing several cheaper, trend-driven items that will quickly go out of style or fall apart.

Consider the cost-per-use of items. For example, that gorgeous pair of boots might seem expensive, but if you wear them frequently, the cost-per-wear becomes quite reasonable. This perspective helps in evaluating the true value of a purchase.

Shop intentionally. When you know exactly what you need, you're less vulnerable to marketing techniques designed to upsell. Do your research, compare prices, and read reviews. This way, you make informed decisions that you won't regret later.

Digital detoxes can be surprisingly effective. Social media can increase the temptation to spend through a barrage of targeted ads and influencer marketing. Limit your screen time or unfollow accounts that trigger unnecessary spending desires.

Also, don't underestimate the joy of experiences over possessions. Allocating funds toward activities, travel, or learning opportunities can be far more fulfilling than acquiring more stuff. Plus, memories created from experiences are priceless keepsakes.

Reward yourself for sticking to your spending plan, but do so in a way that doesn't undermine it. Maybe it's a night out with friends instead of another pair of shoes you don't need. Celebrating your financial discipline reinforces positive behavior.

Lastly, surround yourself with supportive people who respect your financial journey. Money talks can be inspiring when you're with others who share your mindful spending philosophy. When everyone's sipping on the same financial wisdom, it's easier to toast to wise choices.

Remember, financial empowerment is about making choices that fit you - your style, your life, your goals. By incorporating these tips into your spending routine, you can sashay towards financial freedom with a full wallet and a clear conscience.

Chapter 22:
Retirement in Style - Planning
for Your Golden Years

Now that we've laid the groundwork for a strong financial future, it's time to turn our attention to the days when you'll be sipping lemonade on your porch without a care in the world—those golden years. This is the chapter where dreams meet strategy in a dance of numbers and lifestyle choices. Let's pivot our focus to a retirement where style isn't compromised, and leisure is a day-to-day reality. We'll crunch numbers without cringing, and craft plans that feel like a second skin, catering to your every whim and desire. You've spent a lifetime earning your stripes, and now it's about investing in your relaxation and peace of mind. Don't just aim to retire; retire with a flourish that's the envy of your former workplace. We'll weave your passions and interests into a retirement lifestyle plan that's uniquely yours because you're not just retiring from something, you're retiring into everything you've ever wanted. Get ready to redefine retirement, making it just as chic, vibrant, and empowered as every other aspect of your life.

Calculating Your Retirement Needs Transitioning from the buzzing energy of career building to the reflective golden years of retirement marks a significant change. It's not just about the absence of work; it's a lifestyle shift that demands a reinvention of daily structure and a careful consideration of how you'll fund this new chapter.

You've heard it's important to save for retirement, but the question is, how much is enough?

First, let's demystify the process of calculating retirement needs. It might feel overwhelming, but I promise, it's achievable – one step at a time. Imagine retirement as a dream vacation. Just like planning a trip, you need an itinerary; for retirement, that's a detailed financial plan.

To estimate your retirement needs, start with your future budget. Envision your ideal retirement lifestyle – will you go gourmet or grow your own veggies? Are you chasing sunsets across the globe, or enjoying quiet afternoons with grandkids? Your aspirations influence your financial needs, making this visualization a critical starting point.

Once you've pictured your retirement, it's number-crunching time. A common rule of thumb is the '70-80% guideline,' which suggests you will need that percentage of your pre-retirement income annually. Yet, this can be too simplistic. You're unique, and so are your needs. So tailor this to fit your desires, taking into account inflation, healthcare costs, and life expectancy.

Assess your current expenses meticulously. Some will vanish post-retirement, like commuting costs, but others may appear or increase, like medical expenses. Please don't overlook the silent budget eater that is inflation – it'll make your dollars crave a gym session to stay in shape over the years.

Lifespan is a variable we can't control but must consider. With advancements in healthcare, it's not unusual to live well into our 90s. While that's fantastic news, it also means stretching out our savings even further. It's wise to plan for a long life when calculating your needs.

Alright, now pull out those retirement account statements. How much have you saved already? Pat yourself on the back for what you've accumulated, but also cast an eye towards what's still needed. Check your Social Security statements too; while it may not cover all expenses, it's a piece of your financial puzzle.

Now for the technical part – calculating the actual figure. You can use online retirement calculators as a starting point. These tools consider factors like your age, income, savings rate, and expected retirement age to give you a rough estimate. They're not perfect, but they provide a baseline.

Let's not forget about potential healthcare costs. Assume they'll rise because, let's face it, they generally do. And while we're on the topic of costs, remember to factor in taxes. Yes, Uncle Sam will still want a piece of your pie, even in retirement.

You might be wondering about investing to bridge any gaps between your current savings and future needs. Wise investing could potentially yield higher returns, but it also comes with risks. Find a balance that you're comfortable with, considering risk tolerance and investment horizon.

Okay, we've calculated how much we might need, but how do we ensure our money lasts? It's time to strategize withdrawals. The commonly cited 4% rule is a good starting point – the idea being that you can withdraw 4% of your retirement savings annually, adjusting for inflation each year, without running out.

Next, consider how you'll manage unexpected events. Think home repairs, health issues, or supporting a family member. It's not just about saving; it's about being adaptable and having a cushion for the unexpected. A separate emergency fund, even in retirement, is a brilliant move.

But what if you're behind on saving? It's time to fine-tune your priorities and possibly consider working a bit longer, cutting current expenses, or even adjusting your retirement vision. You have the power to course-correct; it's never too late for strategic moves.

To wrap it up, I encourage you to seek professional advice. A financial planner can help customize your retirement strategy, ensuring it aligns with your specific goals and circumstances. They can be invaluable in navigating the complex interplay of savings, investments, and taxes.

Calculating your retirement needs isn't just about the math; it's about creating a vision for your future that's grounded in financial reality. It empowers you to make informed decisions today for a comfortable, fulfilling retirement tomorrow. Embrace this process with enthusiasm and a proactive mindset. With careful planning and determination, you can design a retirement that fits not only your budget but also your dreams.

Creating a Retirement Lifestyle Plan Moving right from crunching retirement numbers to envisioning your post-career life is a must. Crafting a lifestyle plan for retirement means imagining your everyday life in the future and aligning it with financial reality. It's not just about having the resources; it's about making them work for a fulfilling retirement.

Firstly, ask yourself what a satisfying retirement looks like for you. Does it involve travel? Maybe you dream of vineyard tours in France or beach-hopping through the Caribbean. Perhaps you want to contribute to your community, dedicate more time to hobbies, or start a new venture. Define your non-negotiables – those aspects of life that bring you joy and purpose.

Once you've painted a picture of your desired lifestyle, it's time to get practical. What are the costs associated with these pursuits? It's time to budget for fun, darling. It doesn't sound glamorous, but knowing what your dream costs will ground it in reality. Can you afford those cooking classes in Tuscany? If not, what steps can you take now to make them possible?

Now, you might want to shout from the rooftops, "I'm free!" when you retire, but structure can be surprisingly comforting. Think about how you will spend your days. Will you wake up with the sun, take a leisurely morning stroll, and engage in volunteer work? Or perhaps you'll spend mornings with a cup of Earl Grey, knitting or painting before attending a yoga class. Regular activities can provide fulfillment and prevent the retirement blues.

Consider also the importance of social connections. Retirement can lead to a significant shift in your social landscape. Forge a plan to maintain friendships and build new ones. Join clubs, volunteer, or get involved in local politics - whatever floats your boat! Connectivity keeps you vibrant and engaged.

Speaking of staying vibrant, let's not forget wellness. A retirement lifestyle plan is incomplete without a health strategy. What will you do to stay active? How will you manage healthcare costs? Perhaps it's time to explore insurance options or preventative healthcare measures. Remember, a healthy you is a happy you, and health care costs can be a significant part of your retirement budget.

Let's talk housing. Will you downsize, relocate to a retirement community, or move to that beachfront cottage? Each choice comes with financial implications, so weigh the pros and cons and consider how each option fits into your overall plan.

Next, how will you stretch your mind? Retirement is a splendid time to learn. Whether it's history, gardening, or the stock market, commit to lifelong learning. Not only does it keep you sharp, but it can also be an avenue for new social connections and opportunities.

Travel can be one of the most enriching retirement activities. If you plan to globetrot, make sure to account for travel insurance, out-of-pocket expenses, and changing travel needs as you age. Also, consider how often you'd like to travel – is it once a year or are you aiming to be a nomad for a while?

On the flip side, you may find joy in leaving a legacy. This might take the form of giving back through mentoring, creating scholarships, or passing down family history. Calculate these ambitions into your financial plan, as philanthropy can be as much a part of your budget as your grocery bill.

Although it's less glamorous, end-of-life planning is a key part of your retirement lifestyle plan. Ensuring you have an updated will, a healthcare directive, and power of attorney in place can protect you and your loved ones. It's a gift to them to have your affairs in order, and it'll give you peace of mind to enjoy your retirement years fully.

Don't underestimate the power of professional advice. As you transition into retirement and start living off your savings, regular check-ins with a financial planner can help you stay on track. They're not just there for investment advice but can help you adjust your spending as needed to maintain your desired lifestyle.

Finally, be flexible and prepare for the unexpected. No matter how thoughtfully you plan, life can throw curveballs. Your retirement plan should be a living document that evolves with your circumstances and desires.

Creating a retirement lifestyle plan combines dreams with dollars, making for a golden phase that is as golden as you envision. Every step you take today – that course you take, the money you tuck away, the house you downsize to – sets the stage for a retirement filled with zest, purpose, and financial ease. Remember, you're planning for the longest holiday of your life; make it one for the books.

As you loop back to the canvas of your life in retirement, always keep the bigger picture in focus. Blend pragmatism with passion, strategy with soul, and savings with spontaneity. By doing so, you'll ensure not just a comfortable retirement, but one that's rich in experiences, connections, and joy – a lifestyle that's uniquely and beautifully yours.

Chapter 23:
Making Money Moves - Advanced
Wealth Building Strategies

Let's shift gears and delve into the crème de la crème of savvy financial tactics. Think of your financial journey as a masterpiece you're crafting—one that requires not just broad strokes but also attention to intricate details. That's where advanced wealth building strategies come into play. It's about understanding the nuances of financial growth, fine-tuning your investment portfolio to work harder for you while you sleep, and making the most of opportunities that lesser known tax shelters offer. This is your invitation to step up and capitalize on methods that mark the difference between a comfortable nest egg and opulent abundance. So, let's set the stage for some serious wealth amplification, focusing on sophisticated strategies that harness the power of compounding interest, enable smart tax planning, and align your investments with your aspirations for prosperity. Together, we'll turn these techniques into actionable steps for a financial future as dazzling as the most beautifully cut diamond.

Leveraging Compounding for Growth Imagine this: every dollar you invest is a tiny worker, diligently toiling away to plant seeds that will one day grow into a lush forest of wealth. That's the magic of compounding! But let's break it down. Compounding is the process where your investment earnings are reinvested to generate their own earnings. In other words, it's earning interest on interest, and it's a game changer for building wealth over time.

Let's get real: compounding is the best friend you didn't know you needed on your wealth-building journey. You start with saving whatever you can manage, and then, through the wonder of compounding, those savings can bloom into a hefty nest egg over the years. The key here is time; compounding is like a fine wine—it gets better as the years go by. So the sooner you start, the more powerful compounding becomes.

Think about the snowball effect. When you roll a snowball down a snowy hill, it starts small but grows larger as it picks up more snow. Your investments work the same way. The small amounts that you start with pick up size and momentum as the interest they earn gets reinvested and earns more interest. Pretty awesome, right?

Now, you might be thinking, "Okay, that sounds great, but how does it actually work?" Well, imagine you invest $1,000 at an interest rate of 5% per year. In the first year, you'll earn $50 just in interest. By reinvesting that interest, you start the second year with $1,050, and if you earn the same 5%, now you're earning interest on $1,050, giving you $52.50. That might not seem like much more, but over 20 or 30 years, that growth is exponential. Stick with it, and watch your patience pay off!

To truly harness the power of compounding, consistency is your bestie. Regularly investing a fixed amount of money, a practice known as 'dollar-cost averaging', reduces the risk of investing a large amount at the wrong time. Picture it like this: it's like continuously planting seeds throughout the year so you're not betting everything on one season.

But hold on, compounding isn't just for your savings account or your bonds. It works wonders in the stock market too. Dividend reinvestment plans are a fabulous way to automatically use dividends to buy more shares of a stock or mutual fund, trickling into more dividends and even more shares. It's a virtuous circle where your investment portfolio can swell over time.

Patience and discipline are your virtues here. The urge to splurge on that shiny new designer bag can be tempting, but pausing and thinking about how that money could grow might steer you towards investing that cash instead. It's the quiet sacrifices now that can lead to a resplendent financial future.

I know, it can feel like you're not making strides, especially in the beginning when growth seems slow. But that's when it's essential to keep your eyes on the prize and remember the steadfast ally of compounding. Over time, you'll notice the acceleration, and that's when it starts to get really exciting.

What's more empowering than seeing your own money working hard for you, even while you sleep? With compounding, every dollar you save today could become many more dollars in the future. It's about letting your money don the cape and be the superhero in your financial story.

To ensure compounding works its hardest for you, you'll want to minimize fees and taxes, as these can eat into your returns. Look for investment options with low expense ratios and consider tax-advantaged accounts like Roth IRAs or 401(k)s where possible. It's about being savvy and selective with where you grow your money.

Speaking of tax-advantaged accounts, using vehicles like IRAs and 401(k)s is like putting your investments on a fast track. Not only do you benefit from compounding but also from potential tax savings. It's a double-win scenario you'll want to capitalize on!

Compound interest calculators can be incredibly eye-opening. Plug in numbers based on your own situation and see the potential for yourself. Sometimes seeing those figures can be all the motivation you need to stick to your saving and investing plan.

Remember, compounding isn't just about money, it's about time. The more time you allow your investments to compound, the less you have to contribute to reach your goals. It emphasizes the 'start early' philosophy of investing, pushing you to get in the game now, not later.

No matter where you are in your financial journey, it's never too late to make compounding work for you. Whether you're just starting out or you're looking at optimizing your current savings plan, the principles of compounding can always be applied. It's like nurturing a garden; it's always a good time to plant new seeds or to tend to the growth that's already happening.

Inspired yet? Leveraging compounding for growth is about playing the long game and focusing on the future. It means making financial choices that might not give you instant gratification but will set you up for a lavish financial life down the road. It's turning your money into your most loyal and productive employee, working 24/7 to make your dreams a real, tangible future.

So, let's get strategic about how we're saving and investing. Make compounding one of the cornerstones of your wealth-building plan. Your future self will thank you, probably from the deck of her fabulous beach house, funded by the foresight to make compounding a priority early on. And isn't that thought just the motivation we need?

Utilizing Tax Shelters and Loopholes' As you embark on this transformative quest for financial savoir-faire, tax strategies might not be the first thing sparkling on your mind. And yet, understanding the world of tax shelters and loopholes could be likened to discovering a secret garden of savings. It's all about embracing the laws that exist to your advantage without stepping outside the lines of integrity.

Tax shelters—don't let the term mystify you. These are simply investment options or accounts that provide favorable tax treatment. Think of them as VIP rooms where your money can grow with either deferred or zero taxation pressures. These could be retirement accounts like 401(k)s or IRAs, where your contributions can reduce your taxable income now, while you revel in the growth for future lavish retirements.

Loopholes, on the other hand, can be tricky. These are less about specific products and more about approaches or interpretations of tax law that can minimize your overall tax bill. Now, exploiting loopholes sounds naughty, but it's really just about knowing the ins and outs of tax codes and using them to your advantage—completely legally, of course!

For instance, if you're dipping your toes in real estate investments—or already fancy yourself a property connoisseur—there's something called a 1031 exchange. It allows you to defer capital gains tax if you reinvest the proceeds from real estate sales into a like-kind property. It's a splendid way to shuffle your investments without the immediate tax bite.

Charitable contributions are also a dazzling avenue for tax benefits. By donating to registered charities, not only does your heart swell, but so do potential deductions on your tax return. However, to truly benefit from this, you must itemize rather than taking the standard deduction, which means tracking and validating your generous acts is crucial.

Becoming a business owner can open a treasure chest of deductions as well. Be meticulous with your record keeping; those business meals, trips, and even a portion of your home internet costs may decrease your liability at tax time. And if you're one to sail the seas of entrepreneurship, the structure of your business entities can significantly affect your tax situation. S Corps, for instance, may provide opportunities to minimize self-employment taxes. But be cautious—navigating the business tax landscape requires a savvy captain.

Further down the rabbit hole are Health Savings Accounts (HSAs) and Flexible Spending Arrangements (FSAs). These accounts have a tax trinity of benefits: contributions are tax-deductible, the money grows tax-free, and you can withdraw it tax-free for qualified medical expenses. It's the closest thing to a tax hat-trick you can get!

For those juggling family and career, Childcare and Dependent Care Credits can offer some relief. These aren't just deductions; they're credits, which directly reduce your tax bill dollar for dollar. Keep a keen eye on the qualifying expenses and constraints that come with them.

When it comes to investments, capital gains tax can put a damper on your earnings parade. But by holding onto certain investments for more than a year, you move from short-term to long-term capital gains territory, which is typically taxed at a lower rate. Patience can indeed be financially virtuous!

So, how does one stay above board while walking the fine line of tax planning? First, remain informed; tax laws are as fluid as fashion trends—they change with the seasons. Second, engage a trusted tax professional. Unlike a fling with trendy boots, the right advisor is a relationship worth investing in.

And remember, squirreling away money through these methods isn't just about augmenting your bank account—it's about empowering yourself. When you maximize your money's potential, you solidify the foundation of your financial fortress.

While it's tempting to bask in the glow of these strategies, one must also be aware of the shifting sands of regulations. Tax laws can change, and strategies that are perfectly legitimate today may be closed off tomorrow. That's why it's crucial to not just find loopholes, but to understand them deeply—to ensure you're confident and secure in your financial choices.

Lastly, equity in taxes often serves as a hot topic of debate. But whether you're sipping on Merlot or balancing the books, remember that utilizing tax benefits aptly isn't about dodging your part; it's about honoring your intelligence to work smarter with the system in place. It's a testament to your acumen in safeguarding what you've worked so utterly hard to earn.

So, let's toast to being shrewd about taxes. Let's honor the diligence it takes to understand these instruments of wealth preservation. By embracing the art of utilizing tax shelters and loopholes, you become not just a maven of the finer things but also a maestro of monetary management.

Chapter 24:
Legacy and Philanthropy -
Giving Back with Impact

Giving back isn't just about aiding others; it's also about cementing a legacy that reflects our deepest values and passion. Our collective journey through the financial landscape has empowered us with skills and knowledge, allowing wealth to not just flow into our lives, but through them to spark positive change in the world. As we pivot from accumulating wealth to distributing it, we weave the story of our legacy. Philanthropy is more than a withdrawn gesture; it's an active dialogue with society, asking what it needs and how we can provide it with substance and significance. By aligning our charitable contributions with our personal values, we create an impact that resonates and reverberates across communities and generations. Crafting a philanthropic plan isn't a footnote in our financial strategy—it's the crown jewel. It's where strategic planning meets heartfelt giving, where we find tax-smart avenues to bolster our generosity, ensuring our financial intelligence echoes in the causes we champion and in the hearts we touch. As we pen this purpose-drive chapter of our lives, we're not just scribbling in a ledger, but engraving upon the very fabric of humanity.

Charitable Giving and Tax Benefits As we journey deeper into the heart of mindful money management, let's embrace the benevolent aspect of finance. Charitable giving is not only a noble pursuit that can bring about meaningful change; it's also a savvy financial move that garners tax benefits. Now, let's dive into how generosity can harmoniously align with your tax strategy and amplify the positive impact on both your wallet and the world.

Imagine this: with every act of kindness, a portion of your hard-earned money is granted a new life. It's transformed from a mere transaction into a force for good. But that's not all—charity and taxes go hand in hand, like a designer handbag paired impeccably with stilettos. When you contribute to a qualified non-profit organization, you could be eligible for a tax deduction. This effectively reduces your taxable income, potentially leading to substantial savings come April 15th.

Now, to get the full picture, you need to keep in mind itemized deductions. Simply put, these are eligible expenses that you can subtract from your adjusted gross income (AGI). Think of them as the finely detailed beadwork on your financial tapestry. Charitable contributions, when you itemize, can trim down your AGI and might put you in a lower tax bracket, ultimately reducing the amount of tax you owe.

However, not all giving is treated equally in the eyes of the tax world. Be mindful of the qualifications. The charity should be recognized by the IRS, and you'll need to maintain a record of the donation, like a letter from the organization or a bank record. The gift should be purely out of generosity—not for tickets to a gala or merchandise—that portion of your contribution isn't deductible.

Let's talk about limits. In true fashionable sense, more isn't always more. The IRS has a cap on how much you can deduct in a given year, usually a percentage of your AGI. It's essential to stay updated on these limits, as they may change with new tax laws. Consulting with a tax professional can be as vital as enlisting a personal shopper to curate your wardrobe—it ensures that every contribution is accounted for properly.

Moreover, the type of gift matters—cash may be king, but don't overlook non-cash donations. That vintage designer coat you no longer wear? If you donate it, the market value could be deductible. Stock donations can be a powerful move too, allowing you to avoid capital gains tax. Think of it as cutting out the middleman, delivering value straight to the cause whilst fine-tuning your tax liability.

For those who are charitably inclined yet also looking to boost their tax benefits, consider the strategy known as bunching. This tactic involves consolidating charitable contributions you'd make over several years into one larger donation in a single year. This could push you over the standard deduction threshold, making itemizing worthwhile. After the bunched year, you might take the standard deduction in the following years.

Donor-advised funds (DAFs) are another stylish tool in our philanthropic accessory kit, acting as a sort of savings account for charity. You can contribute to the DAF, receive an immediate tax deduction, and recommend grants to your favorite charities over time. This is the equivalent of crafting an investment wardrobe—you're building a legacy of giving that continues to serve your style and substance for years to come.

Let's say your philanthropic soul yearns for large-scale impact, but your current finances are more modest. Volunteering doesn't directly offer tax deductions, but certain expenses incurred, such as travel or uniform costs, are deductible as long as they're necessary for the charity work. It's like paying for the essentials but making a bigger splash with your efforts.

Here's a slice of wisdom—stay organized with your charitable records. Keeping a neat file on your donations is as crucial as organizing your financial documents or your closet. Make it an annual habit to review and tally your charitable acts. Accuracy here is as important as getting the right fit for a cut-to-measure gown.

Excited about leaving a lasting legacy? Consider planned giving techniques, such as bequests or charitable trusts. These are more complex, the haute couture of charity work, but they're worth exploring. They could reduce your estate tax while extending your philanthropic reach beyond your lifetime. Picture that as creating a vintage label, one that speaks to your values for years to come.

Imagine leveraging your retirement accounts for charity too. If you're over a certain age, you might be able to make qualified charitable distributions (QCDs) directly from your IRA. This can satisfy your required minimum distributions (RMDs) without increasing your taxable income—an elegant solution, reminiscent of a sleek, minimalist ensemble that's both practical and profoundly impactful.

Empowerment emanates from informed decisions. Don't let the myriad tax rules intimidate you. The savvy mover understands the landscape or consults someone who does. Each step in charitable giving can be planned to ensure maximum efficiency for tax purposes without ever compromising the purpose or passion behind your generosity.

In wrapping up this chapter, contemplate the bigger picture. The fabric of society gets stronger with every thread of compassion we weave into it. Your charitable efforts, when paired with strategic tax planning, create a tapestry that's not just beautiful but beneficial on multiple levels. Embrace this approach, and you'll steward not only your finances but also your values and vision for a better world.

As we transition into crafting a philanthropic plan that reflects your values, remember the elegance of charitable giving lies not just in the act itself, but in how it fits within the broader design of your financial ensemble. Aim to give with intention, ushering in a ripple effect of kindness, stitched seamlessly into the material of your fiscal strategy.

Creating a Philanthropic Plan that Reflects Your Values
Philanthropy speaks volumes about who you are and what you stand for. It's your legacy, crafted by your passions and beliefs, and a strategic philanthropic plan can ensure that your intentions resonate far and wide. Whether you're a seasoned donor or just beginning to consider how you could contribute to the causes you care about, this plan is your blueprint to making a meaningful impact that aligns beautifully with your heart's intentions.

Firstly, let's demystify what philanthropy means. It's not just about grand gestures or big checks – it's every act of giving that supports causes and communities. Your charitable work, no matter the size or scope, reflects your values and reinforces the change you wish to see in the world. So let's march ahead, with purpose, to channel your generosity in the most effective way.

Start with introspection. What sparks joy and ignites passion within you? Do a deep dive into causes that resonate - be it women's empowerment, education, health, or environmental conservation. Your giving should be a mirror of your life's tapestry - colorful, woven with your experiences, and reflective of your journey.

Once you've identified your core causes, research is your next step. Look into organizations that have a transparent track record of effectiveness and commitment to the issues you hold dear. Reach out to them. Understand their mission and their needs. Philanthropic alignment is much like any relationship – it calls for due diligence to ensure a bond that feels right.

Financial contributions are often the first thought when considering philanthropy. But remember, it's not the only way. Volunteering your time, sharing expertise, or advocating for causes also leave a memorable imprint. Evaluate your lifestyle and decide how you can integrate giving back in a way that's sustainable for you.

It's also wise to consider philanthropy in the context of your budget. It should be a thoughtful line item, not an impulsive add-on. Just like saving and investing for your own future, investing in the future of your philanthropic endeavors demands strategy and foresight.

Setting clear objectives for your giving can add that strategic edge. Define what success means for your philanthropy. Is it a certain number of scholarships funded, trees planted, or families fed? Your objectives will not only guide your actions but also give you a sense of accomplishment as you meet them.

Don't forget that philanthropy can also be integrated into your financial portfolio through socially responsible investing. It's incredibly empowering when your investment decisions reflect your ethical standards and help in promoting social good.

Now, let's talk legacy. Incorporating charitable giving into your estate planning ensures that your values outlive you. Whether it's setting up a scholarship fund or bequeathing assets to a non-profit, these actions solidify your commitment to your causes beyond your lifetime.

Documenting your philanthropic plan is key. It's a living document that charts your course – from the causes you support, the resources you allocate, and the metrics you'll use to measure impact. It keeps you, and potentially your heirs, aligned with the mission you're so passionately dedicated to.

Transparency in your philanthropic endeavors builds trust. Share your journey with those around you - it could inspire collective action and amplify the impact of your work. And when the day comes to pass the torch, ensure that openness remains a hallmark of your philanthropic legacy.

While this all may sound serious – and it is – remember to relish the journey. Celebrate each step, each donation, each moment spent towards bettering the world. Relish the growth that comes from giving and the joy from knowing you're investing in a future reflective of your highest values.

Finally, evaluate and adjust regularly. Staying informed about the issues you care about and the effectiveness of the organizations you support is vital. As the world changes, your philanthropic plan may also need to adapt to remain impactful.

Building a philanthropic plan isn't just about sharing wealth; it's an exercise in sharing your essence. So, as you continue to educate yourself about personal finance and grow your assets, parallelly cultivate your philanthropic vision. It's an integral part of your financial tapestry and a testament to the change you've envisioned for the world. Here's to giving with intention, growing with grace, and leaving a mark that's uniquely yours.

With this philanthropic plan carved out, our journey doesn't end – it merely evolves. As we look forward to further empowering ourselves financially, remember that each choice, each investment, and each act of kindness is a stepping stone to not just your financial independence, but also the upliftment of all around you. This is the essence of true wealth – it blooms and spreads its fragrance, touching lives and transcending time. So let's carry on, armed with savvy and a heart full of grace, ready to write the next beautiful chapter of our financial – and philanthropic – legacies.

Chapter 25:
Financial Independence, Female Empowerment - The Path Ahead

As we look towards the future, let's anchor ourselves in the strength we've harnessed up to this point and embark on this final stretch with heads held high, recognizing the power of financial independence and its crucial role in female empowerment. Imagine a world where we're all making waves, not just in our personal finances but in society at large—where money talk is no longer taboo, and our collective financial savvy lifts us into positions of influence and leadership. This isn't just a dream; it's a horizon that's becoming more reachable by the day as we build networks with trailblazing women rooting for our success. Keep feeding your curiosity and confidence with ongoing learning, because knowledge is that spark that lights the fire of change. Embrace the camaraderie of other fierce, financially literate women marching to the beat of prosperity, and together, let's craft a future where economic resilience is part and parcel of the fabric we weave as empowered women shaping the world.

Continuing Education and Staying Financially Informed
Embarking on the journey to financial literacy is akin to tending to a flourishing garden - it requires regular care, attention, and the acquisition of new knowledge to sustain growth. In today's rapidly evolving financial landscape, staying informed is not just a nice-to-have, it's a must.

Let's start with the undeniable truth that the world of finance never sleeps; it's dynamic and can be overwhelming even for the savviest of investors. But here's where education becomes your power tool, transforming complexities into clarity and anxiety into action. It's about keeping your finger on the pulse of economic trends, market developments, and emerging opportunities and understanding how they impact your financial universe.

Continuing education can come in various forms, none of which require a return to the classroom. The digital age has blessed us with podcasts, webinars, online courses, and a multitude of resources, many geared specifically toward empowering women in finance. Dive into these to not only enhance your knowledge but also to join a community of like-minded individuals who share your drive for financial independence.

Industry newsletters and journals are gold mines for the latest financial insights. Subscribing to reputable financial news outlets can provide a daily dose of economic news that will keep you informed of global market trends and provide interpretative analysis that can help with your own financial decisions.

Books can be your financial mentors in print, covering everything from the basics to the exotic. Don't shy away from bestsellers and new releases, but also consider evergreen classics that cover the foundations of financial wisdom. As the financial sector innovates, your reading list should evolve too, ensuring you're versed in the latest strategies and technologies that shape personal finance.

Conferences, workshops, and seminars are not only informational treasuries but also networking havens. By attending these events, you can learn from industry leaders, gain new perspectives, and connect with peers. The discussions held and connections made at these gatherings often spark new ideas, collaborations, and can greatly propel your financial education.

Don't overlook mentorship. Connecting with a mentor can accelerate your learning curve immensely. A mentor can offer personalized advice, share experiences, and provide support through your financial journey. It's true that in finance, sometimes, the shortcut to knowledge is through someone else's experiences.

Online forums and social media groups dedicated to finance are more than just virtual meeting spaces. They are vibrant communities where you can pose questions, share successes, learn from others' mistakes, and receive support. The collective wisdom of a group who is walking the same path is invaluable.

Technology has equipped us with an array of financial tools and apps designed to make financial education engaging and interactive. Use these tools not just for managing your finances but also for learning purposes. Many apps offer mini-courses and bite-sized lessons that can help you quickly understand complex financial concepts.

Just as you set financial goals, set educational ones too. Having clear objectives such as "understand cryptocurrency basics by Q3" or "learn about estate planning this year" will keep you focused and motivated. Remember, each new piece of knowledge is like a building block in your financial fortress.

Learning doesn't have to be a solo venture. Financial book clubs, study groups, or accountability partnerships can keep you committed to your financial education goals. Discuss what you're learning with peers. This not only solidifies your own understanding but also fosters a shared learning environment.

Personal finance blogs and vlogs offer practical advice and insights into financial trends and personal experiences. Many successful finance bloggers have been where you are and offer relatable advice that can be applied to your own financial strategy.

Remember to filter your sources. Not all information is created equal, and the internet can sometimes lead you down a rabbit hole of misinformation. Stick to trusted, credible sources, and when in doubt, cross-reference information.

Lastly, don't underestimate the power of teaching others. Sharing your knowledge with friends, family, or even through your own blog can reinforce what you've learned. As you articulate concepts to others, you'll solidify your understanding and become more confident in your financial decisions.

An enduring commitment to financial education is what will keep you moving from strength to strength. The financial world won't stand still – and neither should you. Embrace every opportunity for learning as a step towards mastery, independence, and empowerment. Each stride you take adds to a journey not just of personal wealth, but also enrichment and confidence.

Rest assured, this is not where your education ends; this is where it takes flight. So, embrace the vast wealth of knowledge out there, armed with the assurance that every bit you learn is a valuable piece to reinforcing your financial independence and shaping a future that sparkles with possibility.

Joining Forces with Like-Minded Women You've come a long way on this financial journey, and now, as we draw close to the end, it's time to consider the power of unity and collaboration. Joining forces with like-minded women isn't just about building a network; it's about erecting a supportive structure that can propel you towards your financial goals with more strength and speed than you might manage solo.

Think about it—when women come together, there's an undeniable force of energy, education, and empowerment. Round up a group of women passionate about taking control of their financial future, and you've got yourself a powerhouse squad that can tackle any financial challenge that comes their way.

Have you ever felt alone in your financial struggles or achievements? It's a common sentiment among many women, but there's incredible solace and strength in numbers. Creating a financial sisterhood can provide emotional and practical support. Whether you're celebrating a raise or coping with a financial setback, there's a woman out there who understands and can offer empathy or advice.

Embrace women's groups and clubs, either in person or online, that focus on investing, saving, and other financial concerns. These are the spaces where you can share strategies, learn from others' experiences, and keep your finger on the pulse of current financial trends. Think of them as your personal board of directors for money management.

Consider also the role of mentorship. If you've gained some traction in your financial journey, seek to mentor someone who's where you once were. And if you feel you could use some guidance, don't hesitate to reach out to someone you admire for their financial acumen. It's this cyclical mentorship that keeps the community thriving and helps all members, mentors and mentees alike, to grow.

And speaking of growth, networking within professional environments gives you a leg up in your career path. Being surrounded by career-driven women who are also aiming to smash financial ceilings can lead to opportunities otherwise unnoticed. It's not just about swapping business cards—it's about sharing goals, visions, and the tools to turn those aspirations into reality.

Collaboration isn't just for career advancement; it's for investment opportunities as well. Investment clubs—groups of individuals who pool their money to invest in projects, stocks, or real estate—are phenomenal ways to dip your toes into bigger ventures without going in alone. The combined capital and knowledge mitigate some risks and can lead to shared success.

Education is yet another key benefit. Joining a group where financial workshops, seminars, and book clubs are regular occurrences can exponentially increase your financial literacy. You'll likely encounter concepts and products you hadn't considered before, and the group can collectively dissect and analyze these opportunities.

When you align with other women, advocacy and influence become supercharged. Issues like closing the gender pay gap and pushing for workplace policies that support financial equality gain more traction when a group of powerful women stands behind them. There's strength in advocating as a collective rather than just a lone voice.

It's also about lifting as you climb. When you succeed, consider how you can open doors for others. Can you provide financial backing for a woman-started venture, or offer guidance on financial management? Your success story can inspire and direct countless other women towards their own financial triumphs.

On the more personal side, creating accountability groups can boost your likelihood of sticking to your financial plans. Just as workout buddies encourage you to keep fit, financial friends can help you stay on track with savings goals, investing objectives, and debt reduction plans. They're your cheerleaders, your reality check, and sometimes, your tough love when needed.

Let's not forget, either, the enjoyment that comes from social interaction with peers who share your interests. Money talks often come with stress and anxiety, but in the right company, they can become engaging and even fun. Who says you can't discuss Roth IRAs over a glass of wine or compare budgeting apps at a brunch?

Digital platforms have made it easier than ever to find and connect with these supportive networks. Online forums, social media groups, and virtual events bridge geographical divides and bring together women from all walks of life with a common goal: financial empowerment.

As our time together in this book comes to a close, remember that the world outside these pages brims with potential allies on your financial journey. Seek them out, share with them, and grow with them. It's in community and collaboration that women have always thrived—let your financial independence be no different.

So, as you stride forward in your endeavors, keep an open heart and an open mind to the women around you. The path to financial independence and empowerment does not have to be a solitary one. Together, women can not only support and uplift one another but also pave the way for a more equitable financial future for generations to come.

Chapter 26:
Strutting Towards Financial Freedom

As we step forward from the depths of financial uncertainty into the swathes of empowerment, it's impossible not to feel a profound sense of achievement. This journey through the landscape of financial literacy has been transformative, but it's the courage to apply this knowledge that truly leads to freedom. It's like crafting your perfect wardrobe; each piece, from the basic to the bold, comes together to create a look that's unapologetically you. In much the same way, your financial decisions, both big and small, weave together to create a life of security, independence, and prosperity.

Financial freedom isn't just a destination; it's the feeling you get when you realize that you're the one in control of the purse strings. Certainly, you've come to understand that beyond each dollar earned, saved, and invested is the expression of your values, your dedication, and your vision for the future. From setting purposeful goals to crafting a budget that fits like a glove, each stride you've taken has been a pivotal step toward autonomy.

Your budget? It's no longer a dusty old ledger of numbers. It's your ticket to the fashion week of your life – where being practical never goes out of style, and each saving milestone is a trend you've set. You've learned to save with sophistication, mastering the art of stashing cash for the unexpected without sacrificing the joys of today.

Then there's the chic determination with which you've tackled debt. Ah, how elegantly you've begun to unshackle those designer heels from the chains of compounding interest! You've adopted strategies to manage and eliminate debt that work for you because you're not just playing the game; you're rewriting the rules.

And let's not forget the investment avenue, where you've strutted with unwavering confidence. Whether starting small with stocks or diving into the crisp waters of real estate, your portfolio is becoming as diverse and dynamic as your own multifaceted life. You've found your comfort zone in risk versus reward, and you're growing your wealth with each calculated decision.

Retirement planning once seemed a distant thought, but not anymore. Now, you view it as just another fabulous chapter in your life, preparing for it with 401(k)s, IRAs, and ETFs that ensure your golden years are just as golden as you envision. And with a fortified understanding of insurance, you're not just protecting your assets; you're ensuring the continuity of your personal empire.

But this financial runway doesn't just exist in the boardroom or within the silent reflections of a bank account – it thrives in the vibrance of your daily life. You've learned the art of negotiation, rising in your career, and embracing your entrepreneurial spirit, proving that financial rewards await those who speak up.

Taxes, those pesky yet inevitable parts of life, don't intimidate you anymore. You navigate tax season with finesse, understanding that with every deduction claimed, you're safeguarding more of your hard-earned money. Similarly, when it comes to love and money, you've now got the insights to merge finances with your partner while keeping your financial independence intact.

Building generational wealth is no longer a distant dream, but a growing reality. Each decision, from retirement planning to estate planning, is a brick laid in the foundations of a legacy that will endure. And with your heart set on equitable empowerment, you're not only working towards your own freedom but aiding the stride of other women towards theirs too.

The digital age of finance has become your ally. By harnessing the power of financial technology, you've streamlined your savings, investing, and budgeting, all while protecting yourself in the cybernetic world.

The beauty of financial freedom is that it's not a one-size-fits-all ensemble. It's tailored to fit your life's ambitions and contours. Have your ventures into side hustles, international investing, or even cryptocurrency piqued new interests? That's the beauty of this journey – it evolves with you, offering infinite avenues for growth and exploration.

Your voice in advocating for financial equality has grown just as your wealth has. Financial feminism is about raising awareness, challenging norms, and building a future where financial disparities are historic relics. Even through mindful spending, you're practicing financial self-care, honoring your emotional well-being alongside your fiscal health.

As you now stand, ready to color in your own retirement with the hues of your choosing, know that you're no longer just following a set path – you're creating it. Each investment you make, every risk you take, and all the wealth you accumulate is not just for the sake of having more. It's about having the freedom to make choices, to live life on your terms, and to help others do the same.

The world of legacy and philanthropy beckons, inviting you to extend your influence beyond your immediate circle. Your financial success has the power to ripple through communities, fostering change and igniting progress. It's not just about giving back; it's about propelling forward.

So, as you step out, head held high, strutting towards financial freedom, realize you're not walking alone. You're part of a grand movement of women marching together, each to the beat of her own drum, yet in unison towards a future brimming with possibility and prosperity. It's a walk that never truly ends, for with each stride, the path widens, welcoming new travelers and new triumphs.

Remember, this isn't just about the end goal; it's about the empowering strut towards it. Keep learning, keep growing, and keep striding with the undeniable elegance of a woman who knows her worth and is unafraid to claim it. Financial freedom is yours for the taking, one fierce, fabulous step at a time.

Chapter 27:
Financial Terms Glossary

Money talks, and it's high time we speak its language fluently. As you navigate your financial journey, you'll come across jargon that may seem daunting at first. But don't fret. This glossary is here to provide clarity on financial terms that often pop up, especially as you dive deeper into the world of finance. Remember, by understanding these concepts, you'll be better equipped to make informed decisions that help pave the road to financial independence.

A

- **Assets:** Anything of value that you own, which can be converted into cash. This includes real estate, stocks, or even a vintage handbag collection.

- **Amortization:** The process of paying off a debt over time through scheduled, pre-determined installments.

- **Annual Percentage Rate (APR):** The annual rate charged for borrowing or earned through an investment, which includes fees and additional costs.

B

- **Bonds:** A fixed income instrument representing a loan made by an investor to a borrower, often corporate or governmental.

- **Budget:** An estimate of income and expenditure for a set period, helping you to plan your spending and saving.

- **Bull Market:** A financial market where prices are rising or expected to rise, signaling confidence in the economy.

C

- **Capital:** Wealth in the form of money or assets, taken as a sign of the financial strength of an individual, organization, or nation.

- **Compound Interest:** Interest calculated on the initial principal, which also includes all accumulated interest from previous periods.

- **Credit Score:** A number representing an individual's creditworthiness, based on past financial history. This little number can be a big deal when getting a loan.

D

- **Debt:** Money owed by one party to another. Debt can be a powerful tool but must be managed wisely.

- **Diversification:** A strategy that mixes a wide variety of investments within a portfolio. It's like not putting all your designer eggs in one basket.

- **Dividends:** A portion of a company's earnings distributed to shareholders. It's like getting a slice of the profit pie.

E

- **Emergency Fund:** A stash of money set aside to cover the financial surprises life throws your way without derailing your budget.

- **Equity:** Ownership interest in an asset after liabilities are deducted. Think of it as what you truly "own" outright.

- **ETFs (Exchange-Traded Funds):** Investment funds that are traded on stock exchanges, much like stocks. They hold assets such as stocks, commodities, or bonds.

I

- **Income:** The money that you earn, whether through work, investment returns, or business ventures. It's the fuel for your financial engine.

- **Inflation:** The rate at which the general level of prices for goods and services is rising, and subsequently, purchasing power is falling. Simply put, what a dollar bought yesterday, it may not tomorrow.

- **Interest:** The cost of borrowing money or the gain on money saved or invested, serving either as a reward or a fee.

L

- **Liability:** A financial obligation, debt, or claim against you. It's essentially the opposite of an asset.

- **Liquidity:** The ease with which an asset can be converted into cash. Cash is king in the realm of liquidity.

- **Loan:** A sum of money borrowed that is expected to be paid back with interest. It can be the leg up you need if used prudently.

P

- **Portfolio:** A collection of investments held by an individual or institution. It's your financial wardrobe, full of different styles suited for various occasions.

- **Principal:** The original sum of money borrowed in a loan, or the initial amount invested, excluding any earnings or interest.

- **Profit:** The financial gain, especially the difference between the amount earned and the amount spent in buying, operating, or producing something.

R

- **Retirement Accounts:** Savings plans that allow you to set aside money for the golden years, often with tax advantages. Think 401(k)s, IRAs, and more.

- **Risk:** The potential of losing your money when investing. It's the financial world's version of walking in high heels—a balance of poise and caution is key.

S

- **Saving:** The act of reserving income for future use, typically in a safe and accessible form. Start small, think big, and watch your nest egg grow.

- **Stocks:** Securities that represent an ownership share in a company. Holding stocks means you get a piece of the action.

- **Strategy:** Your game plan for how you save, spend, and invest your money. Without strategy, you might just be shooting in the dark.

The financial world is your runway, and knowledge is your most chic accessory. As much as Louboutins can make an outfit soar, understanding these financial terms will help you walk the path to fiscal fabulousness with confidence. Embrace each term as a stepping stone towards mastering your money, because when you're financially literate, you're unstoppable.

Appendix A:
Recommended Reading and Resources

As we close the pages of our financial empowerment journey, it's clear the road doesn't end here. Imagine having a treasure chest filled with jewels of wisdom, tools that carve out paths previously uncharted, and mentors who guide you through the wilderness of wealth-building. That's what you'll find in this curated list of resources - a launching pad for your continued financial exploration.

Unleash Your Money Power: Top Books for Financial Savvy

- **Empower Your Wallet:** Uncover the secrets to thriving financially in a system that often overlooks the unique challenges women face.

- *The Modern Money Manual:* A handy guide brimming with straight-talk advice and actionable tips for managing modern finances like a pro.

- **Invest Like a Queen:** Learn to navigate the stock market with grace and strategy, coming out on top without sacrificing your values or style.

- *Debt-Free Divas:* Stories of women who rocked their debt to zero and the practical steps they took to get there - inspiration and instruction rolled into one.

- **Real Estate, Real Growth:** Property investment can seem daunting, but this read makes it accessible, breaking down barriers and building fortunes.

Podcast Picks: Voices That Inspire Financial Greatness

- **Money Mavens:** These weekly conversations with finance experts will fuel your fire for financial independence and keep you in the loop.

- *Wealth Wizards:* A podcast that captures the essence of transforming your relationship with money - perfect for magic moments of insight while on the move.

- **Startup Stories:** Get a front-row seat to the raw and real journeys of female entrepreneurs who are redefining what it means to build a business.

Online Olympiads: Websites and Forums to Keep You on Your Game

- **Chic Cents:** An online community where wisdom meets whimsy - the perfect place for navigating financial nuances without losing your sparkle.

- *Investor Goddesses:* Here, women from all walks of life discuss strategies, share insights, and support each other's investment endeavors.

- **Safe & Savvy:** This resource is all about keeping your assets protected while exploring the brave new world of fintech and online investments.

Remember, wisdom isn't simply about hoarding information - it's about applying it. As you turn each page and listen to every podcast episode, challenge yourself to convert these nuggets of knowledge into actions that elevate your finances. Blend what you learn with your unique circumstances and watch as you transform into an unstoppable financial force.

There is no final destination on this financial odyssey, only waypoints that mark our growth and success. Continue to expand your library, tune into conversations that matter, and tap into online communities that align with your ambitions. With these resources in hand, your financial narrative will be one of empowerment, abundance, and unapologetic success. And that, my friend, is priceless.

Appendix B:
Worksheets and Checklists for Financial Planning

You've absorbed a wealth of knowledge on your financial journey, from mastering budgeting to exploring sophisticated investment options. Now, let's put that knowledge into practice. In this Appendix, you'll find the essential worksheets and checklists you need to start painting your financial future with broad, confident strokes. These are not mere sheets of paper; they are your map to financial independence and empowerment. Use them to sketch out goals, tally up your triumphs, and keep a keen eye on what lies ahead. Consider these worksheets and checklists your financial planning power tools—crafted to help you sculpt a robust and resilient economic life.

Financial Goal-Setting Worksheet

Begin with clarity on your aspirations—what do you want? This worksheet will guide you through setting SMART goals (Specific, Measurable, Achievable, Relevant, Time-bound). Whether saving up for a swanky getaway or plotting your entrepreneurial empire, nailing down your goals is step one.

Monthly Budget Planner

All that glitters is not gold, and not all expenses are essential. Use this planner to track your income and expenditures meticulously. Hone in on where you can rein in the rampant spending and where you're shining bright and saving right.

Debt Repayment Plan

Don your financial warpaint and get ready to take down debt. This plan will help prioritize which debts to attack first while keeping you motivated as balances melt away—proof that consistency and a rock-solid plan are a debt-slayer's best friends.

Emergency Fund Tracker

Life loves to lob lemons, so let's prepare that lemonade fund. With this tracker, you can calculate your safety net—the cushion that keeps life's bounce less of a bruise.

Investment Portfolio Overview

Show your future some finance love with a well-cultivated investment garden. This overview will help classify your assets and keep tabs on growth—ensuring your money's not just sitting pretty, but growing gorgeously.

Retirement Savings Checklist

The golden years should shine, not stress you out. This checklist will take the guesswork out of retirement planning—leaning on employer benefits, IRAs, and personal savings to make sure your future-self is living her best life.

Insurance Coverage Assessment

Signal to the universe that you've got this life thing covered—literally. From health to home, life to liability, this assessment will ensure you, your possessions, and your loved ones are shielded with the right coverage.

Annual Financial Audit

Year's end is not just a time for toasting success, it's prime time for a financial check-up too. This audit empowers you to look back before you leap forward, tucking away knowledge for future fiscal fortitude.

Now, these tools aren't magic wands, but wield them with wisdom and watch them work wonders. Remember, your finances are personal, as unique as your fingerprint, so tailor your plan, track your progress, and celebrate each milestone with the confidence of a woman who knows her worth and grows it.

With these worksheets and checklists in your financial planning arsenal, you're poised to build not just wealth but a legacy. Embrace the power within these pages and draw up a life that's not just rich, but one that's truly remarkable.

www.ingramcontent.com/pod-product-compliance
Lightning Source LLC
Chambersburg PA
CBHW032001170526
45157CB00002B/493